D1096015

Grand Diplôme® Cooking Course

Volume 14

Grand Diplôme® Cooking Course

A Danbury Press Book

The Danbury Press

a division of Grolier Enterprises, Inc.

Robert B. Clarke Publisher

This book has been adapted from the Grand Diplôme Cooking Course, originally published by Purnell Cookery, U.S.A.

Library of Congress Catalog Card Number: 72-13896

Filmsetting by Petty and Sons Ltd., Leeds, England.
Printed in the United States of America

56789-43210

All recipes have been tested either at the Cordon Bleu Cookery School in London or in our U.S. test kitchens.

Note: all recipe quantities in this book serve 4 people unless otherwise stated.

Contents

From the Editor

Simple foods are the hallmark of traditional **British Cooking** – uncomplicated, satisfying dishes that enhance the flavor of good beef, freshly caught fish and fine vegetables. Sample a rich Scotch broth, flavored with mutton and barley, or a crisp Cornish pasty, filled with a meat and vegetable mixture, that was formerly the miners' substitute for a sandwich. Fruit-filled simnel cake decorated with almond Easter eggs, Welsh buttermilk pancakes made with snow and the famous crumpets and muffins are among the many other British specialties designed for your delectation by the Cordon Bleu Cookery School in London.

You'll find the Continental creations from **French Gâteaux and Pastries** equally delicious and as easily explained in Volume 14 of your Grand Diplôme Cooking Course. Evoke the elegance of gâteau Saint Honoré, a crown of cream puffs filled with a rich pastry cream, or indulge in the sinful extravagance of gâteau au chocolat, filled with chocolate butter cream frosting and topped with crisp curls of chocolate caraque.

Broaden your repertoire with make-ahead **Cold Savory Mousses and Soufflés**, sumptuously rich delicacies that are ideal for a party. And for a truly special occasion, try one of the **Classic Fish Dishes** from France – salmon steaks sauced with tomato hollandaise or trout stuffed with spinach and herbs. Then turn to the pleasures of **Steak Suggestions** and treat yourself to a flaming minute steak in Madeira or a mushroom-stuffed flank steak, with an accompaniment chosen from your second lesson on cooking **Vegetables.**

Finally, apply all of your Grand Diplôme cooking techniques to the varied **Menus** that range from the elegance of chicken suprêmes in a mushroom velouté sauce to the peasant appeal of a chicken and cabbage casserole. A special feature on **Informal Menus** includes ideas for a soup and sandwich snack, a hot and cold buffet, a Provençal dinner, and a simple party supper.

Take a break from your routine recipes and Bon Appétit!

Anne Willan

Cream of spinach soup is garnished with a slice of lemon (recipe is on page 10)

ADD COLOR TO A SIMPLE DINNER WITH SPINACH SOUP

This dinner menu combines simple ingredients in unusual ways – spinach is made into soup, cabbage is baked with chicken in a casserole, and rice is molded in a creamy dessert garnished with pineapple. There's an alternative appetizer as well – gratin of seafood.

The poulet au chou is reminiscent of many Alsatian dishes and suggests a wine in the same tradition. The light, fairly sweet and spicy character of Alsace's Gewürztraminer wine is ideal. In fact, these same qualities make it a good companion for the other courses as well. Several California vintners are now making admirable Gewürztraminer wine that will serve as a worthy alternative to the Alsatian original.

Cream of Spinach Soup
or
Gratin of Seafood

Poulet au Chou
(Chicken Casserole with Cabbage)

Maître d'Hôtel Potatoes

Rice Cream with Pineapple

White wine – Gewürztraminer (Alsace)
or Gewürztraminer (California)

TIMETABLE

Day before
Cut and poach fresh pineapple but do not drain; keep covered in refrigerator.
Make soup and sieve but do not add milk.
Hard cook egg for garnish or make croûtons.

Morning
Roast chicken and partly cook cabbage. Cut up chicken, set on cabbage, spoon over gravy, cover and store in refrigerator ready to complete baking in the evening.
Cook rice for rice cream; drain fresh or canned pineapple and sprinkle over kirsch. Complete, but do not decorate rice mold, cover and keep in refrigerator.
Peel potatoes for duchesse potatoes and keep in cold water.

Assemble ingredients for final cooking from 6:45 for dinner around 8 p.m.

You will find that **cooking times** given in the individual recipes for these dishes have sometimes been adapted in the timetable to help you when cooking and serving this menu as a party meal.

Order of Work
6:45
Boil potatoes for duchesse potatoes.
Whip cream to garnish rice cream and soup (if used).
Unmold rice cream, add garnish and decoration and keep in refrigerator.
7:00
Set oven at moderate (350°F).
Make duchesse potatoes.
7:15
Put chicken casserole to heat and finish cooking.
Cut up cod, arrange in dishes with shrimps and mushrooms.
Make béchamel sauce, spoon over fish and sprinkle with cheese, pipe duchesse potato to border around edge of gratin dishes.
7:30
Bake seafood au gratin.
Boil potatoes for maître d'hôtel potatoes.
Slice lemons or peel and quarter hard-cooked egg for soup (if used).
7:45
Add milk and seasoning to soup and reheat. Heat croûtons in oven (if used).
Drain, peel and complete maître d'hôtel potatoes.
Cook sausages, cut up and add to chicken casserole.
8:00
Turn oven to low and keep chicken and potatoes or *gratin of seafood* hot.
Garnish soup, if you like, and serve.

Appetizer

Cream of Spinach Soup

1 lb fresh spinach
$2\frac{1}{2}$ tablespoons butter
1 shallot, finely chopped
2 tablespoons flour
$2\frac{1}{2}$ cups chicken stock
salt and pepper
$1\frac{1}{2}$ cups milk
pinch of grated nutmeg
2–3 tablespoons heavy cream

For garnish
$\frac{1}{4}$ cup heavy cream, whipped until it holds a soft shape, and $\frac{1}{2}$ lemon cut in thin slices
or 1 hard-cooked egg, peeled and quartered
or croûtons, made from 2–3 slices of bread, crust removed, cut in cubes and fried in 3–4 tablespoons oil and butter, mixed

Method
Remove stems from spinach, and wash thoroughly. Blanch in boiling salted water for 3 minutes to keep the spinach green. Drain and press spinach between 2 plates to remove as much water as possible.

Melt the butter in a pan, add the shallot and cook over low heat until soft but not brown. Blend in the flour and cook, stirring, until straw-colored. Pour in the stock, add the spinach, season and stir until boiling. Cover and simmer 20 minutes.

Strain and reserve liquid and work spinach through a sieve, then stir liquid into the purée; alternatively, purée soup in a blender. Return the soup to the pan, add the milk, bring almost to a boil, taste for seasoning and add nutmeg. Take from the heat and stir in the cream.

To serve the soup, add a spoonful of lightly whipped cream and a slice of lemon to each bowl of soup, or put a quarter of hard-cooked egg in each one, or serve with croûtons in a separate bowl.

Remove the stems from the spinach leaves for soup and wash the leaves before blanching them

Alternative appetizer

Gratin of Seafood

$1\frac{1}{4}$ lb cod fillet or 4 cod steaks
juice of $\frac{1}{2}$ lemon
1 cup ($\frac{1}{4}$ lb) mushrooms, sliced
1 cup ($\frac{1}{2}$ lb) small cooked, peeled shrimps
béchamel sauce, made with 2 tablespoons butter, 2 tablespoons flour, $1\frac{1}{2}$ cups milk (infused with slice of onion, 6 peppercorns, blade of mace and a bay leaf)
salt and pepper
2–3 tablespoons grated Parmesan cheese
duchesse potatoes (for serving)

4 individual gratin dishes

Method

Set oven at moderate (350°F) and butter the gratin dishes.

Cut cod into strips or chunks, discarding skin and bones. Spread cod in prepared dishes and sprinkle with lemon juice. Scatter the sliced mushrooms and shrimps over the cod.

Make béchamel sauce, season well, spoon the sauce over the fish and sprinkle with Parmesan cheese. Pipe a border of duchesse potatoes around the gratin dishes. Bake in heated oven for 20–25 minutes or until golden brown.

Accompaniment to alternative appetizer

Duchesse Potatoes

Over medium heat, mash 3–4 medium-sized boiled potatoes with $\frac{1}{2}$ cup milk, 2–3 tablespoons butter and seasoning until light and smooth. Take from the heat, beat in 1–2 egg yolks and spoon into a pastry bag fitted with a large star tube. Pipe a border around the chosen dish. Brush the piped border with 1 egg, beaten with $\frac{1}{2}$ teaspoon salt, to glaze.

Cooked peeled shrimps, cod and mushrooms form the basis of gratin of seafood

For poulet au chou, serve pieces of roast chicken on a bed of cabbage garnished with slices of sausages or frankfurters

Entrée

Poulet au Chou
(Chicken Casserole with Cabbage)

$3\frac{1}{2}$–4 lb roasting chicken
1 medium, firm head of green cabbage, shredded
5 tablespoons butter
salt and pepper
1 cup chicken stock
$\frac{1}{2}$ lb salt pork, cut into lardons
1 onion, sliced
1 tart apple, pared, cored and sliced
1 cup cider
$\frac{1}{2}$ lb country sausages or frankfurters
1 tablespoon chopped parsley (for garnish)

Trussing needle and string

Method

Set the oven at hot (400°F).

Put 1 tablespoon butter inside the chicken, sprinkle the inside with salt and pepper, truss the chicken and rub 2 tablespoons more butter on the outside.

Set the chicken, breast side up, in a small roasting pan, pour around $\frac{3}{4}$ cup stock and roast chicken in the heated oven 40–45 minutes, basting often and turning bird so it is thoroughly browned on all sides.

Blanch the lardons in boiling salted water for 2 minutes and drain them.

In a flameproof casserole heat remaining 2 tablespoons butter, add the onion and lardons and cook until just beginning to brown. Add the cabbage and apple with plenty of seasoning and stir to mix well. Pour over the cider and cover with thickly buttered foil and the lid. Bring to a boil on top of the stove, then bake in heated oven – or in a separate oven at moderately hot (375°F) – for about 20 minutes. Take out and pour off and reserve cooking liquid.

Cut the chicken into 5 serving pieces, discarding the backbone, and set the chicken on top of the cabbage. Discard any fat from the roasting pan and deglaze the pan juices with the reserved cabbage liquid and remaining stock. Season well and strain gravy over chicken. Cover casserole, lower oven heat to moderate (350°F) and continue baking for 20–30 minutes or until the chicken and cabbage are very tender.

Broil the country sausages until browned or simmer the frankfurters in water for 6–8 minutes or until cooked. Cut the sausages or frankfurters in diagonal slices and arrange them around the chicken. Sprinkle the dish with parsley and serve in the casserole, with maître d'hôtel potatoes separately.

> **Lardons** of salt pork or bacon, cut in $\frac{3}{4}$ X $\frac{1}{4}$ X $\frac{1}{4}$ inch chunks, are added to casseroles and garnishes for flavor. They are usually blanched before using. In French 'lard' means bacon.

Add the shredded cabbage and sliced apple to the lightly browned onions and lardons

Arrange the partly cooked chicken pieces on top of the cabbage and apple mixture

Accompaniment to entrée

Maître d'Hôtel Potatoes

$1\frac{1}{2}$ lb even-size medium potatoes
2 tablespoons butter
1 shallot, chopped
2 tablespoons chopped parsley
salt and pepper

Method

Scrub the potatoes and boil them in their skins for 15–20 minutes or until tender but still firm. Drain, and peel them and cut into three-eighth inch slices; arrange them, overlapping, in a hot shallow ovenproof dish and keep warm.

Melt the butter in a small pan, add the shallot, cover the pan and cook over a low heat for 2–3 minutes or until shallot is soft. Take from the heat, stir in parsley and plenty of salt and pepper and pour over the potatoes. Heat in a moderate oven (350°F) for 3–5 minutes before serving.

Note: if serving gratin of seafood as the appetizer, omit maître d'hôtel potatoes with the entrée.

Rice Cream with Pineapple

1 fresh pineapple or 1 can ($14\frac{1}{2}$ oz) pineapple slices
1–2 tablespoons kirsch
$\frac{1}{4}$ cup sugar syrup (made with $1\frac{1}{2}$ cups water and $\frac{1}{2}$ cup sugar) if using fresh pineapple, or $\frac{1}{4}$ cup water or canned pineapple juice

For rice cream
$\frac{1}{3}$ cup rice
4 cups milk
1 vanilla bean or 1 teaspoon vanilla extract
3 tablespoons sugar
1 egg yolk
1 envelope gelatin
$\frac{1}{2}$ cup heavy cream, whipped until it holds a soft shape

For decoration
$\frac{1}{2}$ cup heavy cream, stiffly whipped (optional)
candied violets and angelica, or candied cherries or candied pineapple

Ring mold (1 quart capacity)

Method

Lightly oil the mold.

To prepare fresh pineapple and sugar syrup: wash the pineapple, cut away the skin and eyes, then slice it and remove the core. Soak the pineapple skin and core in the $1\frac{1}{2}$ cups of water for about 30 minutes to give flavor. Strain this water onto the $\frac{1}{2}$ cup sugar in a pan, and heat gently until the sugar is dissolved. Bring to a boil, add the pineapple slices and poach 10–15 minutes or until the slices are transparent. Cool and drain the slices, reserving the liquid. If using canned pineapple slices, drain them but do not cook. Sprinkle them or poached fresh slices with kirsch.

To make rice cream: rinse the rice in a strainer under cold running water until the water is clear. Put rice in a large pan with the milk and vanilla bean (if using) and simmer over moderate heat, stirring frequently, for about 35 minutes or until rice is tender and milk is almost absorbed. Remove vanilla bean.

Watchpoint: the rice mixture should look creamy at this point and fall easily from a spoon; do not let it overcook until dry.

Mix sugar into rice and let cool a little. Stir in egg yolk and vanilla extract, if using. Sprinkle gelatin over pineapple juice, or syrup or water, and let stand 5 minutes until spongy, then dissolve it over a low heat. Stir into rice and chill. When mixture is cold and starts to set, fold in $\frac{1}{2}$ cup lightly whipped cream. Spoon rice cream into prepared mold and chill 2 hours or until set.

To serve, unmold the rice cream, cut pineapple slices in half and arrange around mold. Chop remaining pineapple and pile it into center of mold. Decorate with rosettes of whipped cream, if you like, topped with candied violets and angelica, or candied fruits.

Stir the egg yolk into the cooked and sweetened rice, after letting it cool slightly

Top the rosettes of whipped cream with candied violets and diamonds of angelica

Rice cream, with pineapple sprinkled with kirsch, whipped cream and candied violets, makes an attractive dessert

Zucchini and eggplant au gratin (recipe is on page 20)

COOKING WITH VEGETABLES (2)

In the days before refrigeration, the first spring vegetables were hailed as a welcome relief from the winter monotony of roots like potatoes and carrots and the occasional cabbage. Today, when a wide range of young vegetables remains available throughout the winter, we can enjoy their sweet flavors and brilliant colors all year round. To be at their best, vegetables should be cooked only until just tender, and green vegetables should be refreshed with cold water to 'set' the bright colors.

Lima beans and baby carrots are mixed together in poulette sauce for lima beans Marie-Anne

Lima Beans Marie-Anne

2 cups shelled baby lima beans
½ lb baby carrots
1 tablespoon butter

For poulette sauce
2 tablespoons butter
2 tablespoons flour
1½ cups well-flavored chicken stock
salt and pepper
1 egg yolk
2–3 tablespoons heavy cream
½ teaspoon savory
1 tablespoon chopped parsley

Serve with lamb and veal.

Method

Cook the beans in boiling salted water for 15–20 minutes or until just tender, drain, refresh and drain again. If the carrots are large, quarter them; cook in boiling salted water for 15 minutes or until just tender and drain them. In a saucepan or flameproof casserole melt butter, add beans and carrots, cover and keep warm.

To make poulette sauce: melt butter, stir in the flour and cook over medium heat until the roux is pale straw-colored. Take from heat, pour in stock, then bring to a boil, stirring. Season to taste and simmer 2–3 minutes or until sauce is the consistency of heavy cream. Mix egg yolk with the cream, stir in a little of the hot sauce and stir this liaison with the herbs back into remaining sauce.

Heat the sauce until it thickens slightly but do not let it boil. Pour it over the beans and carrots and heat them, until very hot, shaking pan so sauce and vegetables mix well. Serve in the casserole or transfer to a hot serving dish.

New Potatoes

The following recipes for small new potatoes are good for serving with roasts, steak or chicken. If you like, serve the potatoes in individual baking dishes or casseroles.

New potatoes may be peeled by scraping with a brush or pot scrubber before cooking, or they can be peeled with a knife after boiling. The recipes here can also be used for large potatoes; cut them into four and remove the sharp edges with a peeler or small knife. Large potatoes do not have as much flavor as small new ones.

Potatoes Duxelles

10–12 small new potatoes

For sauce
3 tablespoons butter
$\frac{1}{2}$ small onion, finely chopped
1 cup ($\frac{1}{4}$ lb) mushrooms, finely chopped
1$\frac{1}{2}$ tablespoons flour
2 cups well-flavored chicken or veal stock
$\frac{1}{2}$ bay leaf
salt and pepper
2 teaspoons chopped mint or parsley

Method

Wash and scrape potatoes, cook them in boiling salted water for 10–15 minutes or until just tender and drain. Or, if you prefer, boil them in their skins and then peel them.

To make the sauce: melt the butter, add the onion and cook gently until soft but not browned. Add the mushrooms and cook over high heat until all the moisture has evaporated. Stir in the flour, pour in the stock and bring to a boil, stirring. Add the bay leaf and seasoning and simmer 6–8 minutes or until the sauce is the consistency of heavy cream.

Drain potatoes and peel them if they have not already been scraped. Remove bay leaf and add potatoes to the sauce. Reheat, add the mint or parsley and shake the pan to mix potatoes and sauce thoroughly. Taste for seasoning.

Potatoes with White Wine

10–12 small new potatoes
$\frac{1}{2}$ cup white wine
3 tablespoons butter
salt and pepper
1$\frac{1}{2}$ tablespoons chopped mixed herbs (parsley, mint and thyme)

Method

Scrape the potatoes and cook them in boiling salted water for 10–15 minutes or until tender or, if you prefer, boil them in their skins, then drain and peel them. Return the potatoes to the pan and pour over the wine while they are still hot. Boil rapidly until the wine is reduced to 2 tablespoons.

Watchpoint: be sure the wine is well reduced almost to a syrup before adding the butter or the potatoes will be too moist.

Add the butter to the pan in 2–3 pieces, off the heat, then heat gently, shaking the pan until the butter is melted. Add seasoning and herbs and transfer the potatoes to a hot serving dish.

Peas Bonne Femme

3–4 cups shelled fresh peas
4 slices of bacon, diced
6 scallions, trimmed and cut in half
1 Bibb lettuce or 1 Boston lettuce heart, coarsely chopped
1 cup veal or chicken stock
salt and pepper
sprig of mint (optional)
kneaded butter (made with 1 tablespoon butter, 1$\frac{1}{2}$ teaspoons flour)

Serve with roast duck or chicken.

Method

Blanch the bacon in boiling water for 1 minute and drain. In a saucepan or flameproof casserole fry bacon and scallions together until lightly browned. Add lettuce, peas and stock, season and bring to a boil. Add the mint, if used, cover the pan and simmer 12–15 minutes or until the peas are just tender.

Take the pan from the heat and add the kneaded butter in small pieces. Shake the pan or stir very gently until the kneaded butter melts and blends, then bring to a boil so the mixture thickens slightly. Discard the mint, adjust seasoning and transfer peas to a hot serving dish.

To Refresh Vegetables
Pour cold water over previously cooked and drained green vegetables to 'set' their colors. (Meats and variety meats may be refreshed in the same way to clean after blanching.)

Turnips with Onions

6–8 small white turnips
3 medium onions, sliced
$\frac{1}{4}$ cup butter
salt
black pepper, freshly ground

Serve as an accompaniment to roast and broiled meats, and with capon and turkey.

Method

Peel and cut the turnips in $\frac{1}{4}$ inch slices. Cook in boiling salted water for 10–15 minutes or until just tender and drain. Cook the onions in the butter over medium heat until lightly browned. Add them to the turnips with seasoning and mix gently.

Caramelized Tomatoes

4–5 tomatoes, halved
salt and pepper
3 tablespoons browned breadcrumbs
2 tablespoons dark brown sugar
2 tablespoons melted butter

Serve with steak, roast meats and omelets.

Method

Set tomatoes, cut side up, in a buttered baking dish, season and bake in a moderate oven (350°F) for 7–10 minutes.

Mix breadcrumbs and sugar together and stir in the butter. Sprinkle this mixture over the tomatoes and continue baking in a hot oven (425°F) for 6–8 minutes or broil them until browned and the sugar is slightly caramelized.

Stuffed Tomatoes Valaisanne

4 large tomatoes

For cheese filling
2 tablespoons grated Gruyère cheese
1 cup milk
pinch of cayenne
pinch of nutmeg
2 tablespoons butter
2 tablespoons flour
salt and pepper
3 egg yolks
3 egg whites
2 teaspoons chopped chives
$\frac{1}{4}$ cup white wine

This dish makes an excellent appetizer or the tomatoes can be served as an accompaniment to fish, chicken and veal.

Method

Peel the tomatoes, cut a thin slice from each stem end and discard it. Scoop out and discard the seeds. Turn the tomatoes upside down on a plate and let drain well.

To make cheese filling: scald milk with cayenne and nutmeg. In a saucepan melt the butter, stir in the flour off the heat and pour in the scalded milk. Bring to a boil, stirring, season well and simmer 2 minutes. Take from the heat and beat in the egg yolks, one at a time. Add the cheese, taste for seasoning, cover and let cool until still fairly hot to the touch.

Beat the egg whites until they hold a stiff peak and fold them as lightly as possible into the cheese sauce.

Season the insides of the tomatoes, sprinkle with half the chopped chives and set them, touching each other, in a small baking dish. Sprinkle them with the white wine and fill them with the cheese mixture.

Bake the tomatoes in a moderate oven (350°F) for 20 minutes or until the filling is slightly puffed and brown and tomatoes are just cooked. Sprinkle over remaining chives just before serving.

Spinach Galette

$1\frac{1}{2}$ lb fresh spinach
$\frac{1}{4}$ cup light cream
3 tablespoons butter
4 large eggs, beaten to mix
salt and pepper
1 tablespoon grated Parmesan or Gruyère cheese

For tomato coulis
3 tomatoes, peeled, seeded and sliced
1 tablespoon butter
8–10 scallions, cut in pieces
2 teaspoons flour
$\frac{1}{4}$ cup stock (optional)

Serve as an appetizer or a light supper dish.

Method

Wash spinach, remove the stems and cook it in boiling salted water for 5–6 minutes. Drain well and press between 2 plates to extract all the water. Work the spinach through a sieve and add the cream or purée in a blender with the cream. Melt 1 tablespoon of the butter, stir it into the purée with the eggs and season well.

Watchpoint: the finished galette mixture should be the consistency of thick pancake batter.

To make tomato coulis: melt the butter, add the scallions and cook until just tender. Stir in the flour, off the heat, add the tomatoes and seasoning. Cover the pan and cook over low heat until the mixture is pulpy, adding the stock if the mixture seems dry.

To cook the galette: in a 5–6 inch skillet or frying pan melt 1 tablespoon butter, add enough spinach mixture to make a $\frac{1}{4}$ inch layer and cook over fairly low heat for $1\frac{1}{2}$–2 minutes or until the galette is set. Turn over, cook 10 seconds on the other side and set galette in the center of a warm serving dish.

Spread the galette with a spoonful of tomato coulis and keep warm. Cook the remaining mixture the same way, adding more butter to the pan when necessary, and pile the galettes one on top of another, layering them with coulis. Pour remaining coulis around galettes, sprinkle top with grated cheese and cut in wedges like a cake for serving.

Zucchini and Eggplant au Gratin

$\frac{1}{2}$ lb small zucchini, thinly sliced
1 large or 2 medium eggplants, sliced
salt
$\frac{1}{4}$ cup oil
black pepper, freshly ground
$\frac{1}{2}$ cup grated Parmesan cheese
$\frac{1}{2}$ cup fresh white breadcrumbs

Method

Sprinkle the eggplants with salt and let stand 30 minutes to draw out the bitter juices (dégorger). Rinse them with cold water, then drain them thoroughly.

Brush both sides of the eggplant slices with oil and arrange them, overlapping, in a shallow baking dish. Spoon over the remaining oil, sprinkle with pepper, then with a mixture of the cheese and breadcrumbs. Bake the eggplants in a moderate oven (350°F) for 25–30 minutes or until they are tender and browned.

Cook the zucchini in boiling salted water for 4–5 minutes or until just tender, drain and arrange them, overlapping, around the edge of the dish.

Vegetables (2)

Stuffed tomatoes Valaisanne make an excellent appetizer

Creamed Beets

6–8 small beets
1 tablespoon butter
1 tablespoon grated fresh horseradish or 2 tablespoons prepared horseradish
1–2 tablespoons heavy cream
salt and pepper

For white sauce
2 tablespoons butter
2 tablespoons flour
1½ cups milk

Serve with roast or corned beef.

Method

Scrub the beets and trim the stems but do not cut the roots. Cook in boiling salted water for 30–40 minutes or until the skins rub off easily with your fingers. Drain the beets, rinse them under cold water until cool enough to handle, trim the roots and slip off the skins. Melt the butter in the pan, replace the beets and keep warm.

Make the white sauce and simmer it to the consistency of heavy cream. Add the horseradish and cream and season to taste. Transfer the beets to a warm serving dish and coat them with sauce.

Stuffed Eggplant with Olives

6 baby eggplants
12–15 ripe olives, pitted and chopped
6 tablespoons olive oil
¼ cup butter
½ cup fresh white breadcrumbs
1 tablespoon chopped parsley
4 anchovy fillets, chopped
2 tablespoons capers
salt and pepper
1 teaspoon oregano
1 lb Italian-type plum tomatoes, peeled, seeded and cut in strips
2 red bell peppers, cored, seeded, cut in strips and blanched
½ lb sliced Mozzarella or Bel Paese cheese

Method

Wipe the eggplants, trim the stems and cut in half, lengthwise. Sprinkle them lightly with salt and leave 30 minutes to draw out the juices (dégorger). Rinse the halves with cold water and dry on paper towels.

In a large skillet heat 4 tablespoons of the oil and fry the eggplant halves, cut sides down, over fairly low heat until they are browned. Scoop out the flesh of the eggplants and chop it. Reserve the shells.

In a pan melt the butter, add the olives, breadcrumbs, parsley, anchovies and capers and fry gently, stirring, until the crumbs are lightly browned. Season, add the oregano and remaining olive oil and stir in the eggplant flesh.

Set oven at moderate (350°F).

Fill the eggplant shells with the stuffing, smooth the tops and place a few strips of red pepper and tomato on each half.

Lightly oil a baking dish or roasting pan, set the eggplant halves in it, brush each one with a little melted butter and bake in heated oven for 30 minutes or until the eggplants are very tender.

Five minutes before serving, top each eggplant half with a slice of cheese, turn up the oven to very hot (450°F) and bake the eggplants until the cheese is melted, or melt it under the broiler, if you like.

Green Beans with Pine Nuts

1 lb green beans
½ cup pine nuts
2 tablespoons butter
1 tablespoon chopped parsley
salt and pepper

Serve with roast lamb and chicken.

Method

Trim the beans and leave them whole, if they are small, or halve them if they are large. Cook them in boiling salted water for 10–15 minutes or until just tender, drain, refresh and drain again.

Melt the butter, add the beans and pine nuts; cook over medium heat, tossing the beans carefully, until very hot and well coated with butter. Add parsley and seasoning and pile the beans in a hot serving dish.

Sautéed Fennel

2 large bulbs of fennel
5 tablespoons butter
salt and pepper
grated rind and juice of ½ lemon
1 tablespoon chopped parsley
1 teaspoon mixed herbs (thyme, oregano, basil)

Serve with baked fish.

Method

Wash the fennel, trim the stalks and roots and cut in thick slices.

In a skillet melt 3 tablespoons butter, add the fennel and seasoning, cover and cook gently, shaking the pan occasionally, for 5–6 minutes or until the fennel is just tender. Remove lid and cook over high heat until all moisture is evaporated; transfer to a warm serving dish.

Wipe out the pan, add the remaining butter and cook to a noisette (nut-brown); at once add the lemon rind and juice with the herbs and seasoning and pour the butter while still foaming over the fennel, and serve.

Fennel is a bulbous white root that looks a little like a fat celery heart. It is related to herb fennel and has a pleasant flavor of anise.

Sautéed fennel with noisette butter makes an interesting accompaniment for baked fish

Strip steak Provençale is garnished with a salpicon of olives, peppers, onions and eggplant (recipe is on page 26)

SUGGESTIONS FOR STEAK

A steak is only as good as the steer it came from and only top quality steak, graded Prime or Choice by the U.S. Department of Agriculture, should be broiled or pan fried. Add seasoning, perhaps a few chopped herbs or a simple sauce and, with a vegetable or two, you have a simple but superb dinner. No amount of clever cooking can upgrade an inferior steak, so choose the best for broiling and keep the less expensive cuts for stewing or braising.

Strip Steak Provençale

4 strip steaks, 1–1½ inches thick
1 tablespoon oil
salt and pepper

For salpicon
1 medium eggplant, sliced
¼ cup olive oil
1 large onion, sliced
2 red bell peppers, cored, seeded, cut in strips and blanched
1 green pepper, cored, seeded, cut in strips and blanched
12–16 small ripe olives, preferably Greek-style, pitted

For sauce
2 shallots, chopped
2 teaspoons tomato paste
½ cup white wine
¼ cup stock

Method

To prepare salpicon: score the eggplant slices, sprinkle with salt, leave 30 minutes to draw out the juices (dégorger), then rinse and dry on paper towels.

In a skillet heat the ¼ cup of oil and fry onion until browned. Add the peppers and shake the pan until they are thoroughly heated. Remove and keep warm. Add eggplant slices and fry gently until tender and brown all over. Put back the onion and pepper mixture, add the olives, season and keep hot.

In a large skillet, pan fry the steaks in the oil over high heat, allowing 3 minutes on each side for rare steak. Sprinkle steaks with seasoning just after turning over, and lower the heat to medium once steaks are brown on both sides. When cooked, arrange steaks on a platter, spoon the salpicon on top and keep warm.

To make sauce: add shallot, tomato paste, wine and stock to the steak skillet and bring to a boil. Spoon over steaks and salpicon and serve.

Provençale dishes are made with the vegetables characteristic of the Provence region in southern France such as tomatoes, peppers and eggplant. Often garlic and olives are included for flavoring.

Minute Steak with Madeira

4 thin entrecôte steaks or 8 thin fillet steaks
¼ cup Madeira
2 tablespoons bacon drippings or oil
salt
black pepper, freshly ground
2 onions, sliced
1 cup stock

Method

In a skillet heat the drippings or oil and fry steaks over high heat, allowing 1 minute on each side for rare steak; sprinkle them with seasoning. When cooked, remove steaks and keep warm.

In the skillet, fry onion until brown, put back the steaks, add the Madeira and flame. Remove the steaks, arrange on a platter and keep warm.

Add stock to the pan, boil until it is reduced and well flavored, taste for seasoning and spoon it over the steaks. Serve with rice pilaf and zucchini.

Steak Pizzaiola

3 lb piece sirloin steak, 1½ inches thick
3 tablespoons olive oil
5–6 tomatoes, peeled, seeded and cut in strips
2 cloves of garlic, crushed
1 tablespoon chopped parsley
1 teaspoon oregano or basil
salt
black pepper, freshly ground

Fresh Italian-type plum tomatoes will give the authentic full flavor to this dish, although it is also good with regular tomatoes.

Method

In a frying pan heat 2 tablespoons oil, add tomatoes, garlic, herbs and seasoning and cook quickly for 1–2 minutes, stirring constantly. The tomatoes should be just cooked but must not become pulpy.

In a heavy skillet or frying pan, heat the remaining oil and pan fry the steak over high heat, allowing 4–5 minutes on each side for rare steak.

Turn the heat down to medium once the steak is well browned. Sprinkle the steak with seasoning after turning over.

When cooked to taste, spoon the tomato mixture on top of the steak, cover the pan, lower heat and cook gently for 5 minutes. Serve with a green salad and buttered noodles, if you like.

Minute Steak Soubise

4 thin entrecôte steaks or 8 thin fillet steaks
5 tablespoons butter
3 large onions, thinly sliced
1 cup red wine
1 cup light cream
salt
black pepper, freshly ground
1 teaspoon arrowroot (mixed with ¼ cup well-flavored stock)

Method

In a pan melt 2 tablespoons of the butter, add onion and fry slowly until golden brown. Add half the wine and continue cooking slowly for 8–10 minutes. Drain onion, reserving liquid; arrange down the center of a heated platter and keep warm.

In a skillet melt remaining butter and fry steaks over high heat, allowing 1 minute on each side for rare steak. Arrange the steaks on a bed of onion and keep warm.

Add the remaining wine to the skillet, boil to dissolve the pan juices and add the reserved liquid from the onion. Add the cream and seasoning. Stir arrowroot into sauce and bring just to a boil. Spoon a little sauce over the steak and serve the rest separately.

Soubise refers to finely sliced or puréed onions, usually mixed with rice, seasonings, butter and cream. A cream sauce may be used instead of rice.

For Garrick steak, slit a pocket in the steak and stuff with a mushroom and ham filling

Garrick Steak

2–3 lb top round steak or flank steak
1–2 tablespoons oil
parsley butter (for serving)
bunch of watercress (for garnish)

For mushroom stuffing
1 cup ($\frac{1}{4}$ lb) finely chopped mushrooms
1 tablespoon butter
1 shallot, finely chopped
$\frac{1}{2}$ teaspoon thyme
1 tablespoon chopped parsley
$\frac{1}{4}$ cup finely chopped ham
2 tablespoons fresh white breadcrumbs
salt and pepper

Trussing needle and string or poultry pins

The Garrick is a famous club in London where this steak is a specialty.

Method
To prepare the mushroom stuffing: in a skillet heat butter and cook shallot until soft. Add mushrooms, cover and cook over low heat for 4–5 minutes until mushrooms are soft. Stir in the herbs, ham, breadcrumbs and plenty of seasoning. Cool and reserve.

Slit steak from one side almost to the other side to form a pocket and fill with the mushroom stuffing. Sew up with trussing needle and string, or secure with poultry pins, brush with oil and broil 5–6 minutes on each side for rare steak. Remove string or poultry pins and arrange steaks on a platter, sprinkle with seasoning and keep hot.

To serve, cut the round steak diagonally in $\frac{1}{2}$ inch slices and the flank in very thin diagonal slices. Make parsley butter and pour over the steak. Garnish with watercress and serve with Parisienne potatoes.

Note: if the meat is of top quality, it can be broiled as described. Otherwise it should be browned on both sides in a skillet, then braised in a moderate oven (350°F) in a covered pan with wine or stock and root vegetables for 1–1$\frac{1}{2}$ hours or until the meat is very tender. Then drain and pour over parsley butter.

Parsley Butter

Melt $\frac{1}{4}$ cup butter in a small pan and when lightly browned, at once take from the heat and add 1 tablespoon chopped parsley and a dash of Worcestershire sauce or squeeze of lemon juice. Use immediately.

Steak au Poivre

4 steaks (Porterhouse, strip, fillet or entrecôte), 1 inch thick
$\frac{1}{4}$ cup cracked black pepper
2–3 tablespoons oil
noisette butter (for serving)
bunch of watercress (for garnish)

Method
Brush steaks with oil and press cracked pepper on both sides; leave 1–2 hours.

Broil 5 minutes on each side or pan fry for 3 minutes on each side for rare steak. Transfer to a platter and keep warm.

Make noisette butter, pour over steaks and garnish them with watercress. Serve with broiled tomatoes and a green salad.

Some people like to eat the cracked pepper, others prefer to scrape it from the steak because the meat is already well-flavored from cooking with it.

Noisette Butter

In a small pan heat $\frac{1}{4}$ cup butter and cook to a nut-brown (noisette). At once add the juice of $\frac{1}{2}$ lemon and use immediately.

Salmis of duck is garnished with sausages and olives; fried croûtes are arranged around the dish (recipe is on page 32)

ROAST DUCK WITH A DIFFERENCE

Start your dinner menu with a mold of shrimps layered with tomato and garnished with celery or watercress. Then serve a salmis of duck with a rich sauce. For dessert, there is a pie of poached apples with a decorative crust.

As an accompaniment for rich fowl and game dishes, the white wines of France's Rhône valley are less well-known than the reds. But from Hermitage, a picturesque hillside vineyard halfway between Lyon and the Mediterranean, comes a white wine with strength to match the richness of the duck and a more feminine fragrance to suit the white wine sauce.

A markedly different wine, but one which also combines authority with a special bouquet, is the Diamond – a traditional white from New York's Finger Lakes District.

Couronne of Shrimps in Aspic

Salmis of Duck
with Olives
New Potatoes *Green Peas*

Tarte aux Pommes Grillée
(Latticed Apple Pie)

White wine – Hermitage (Rhône)
or Diamond (New York)

TIMETABLE

Day before
Prepare stock for salmis of duck and couronne of shrimps. Clarify aspic for couronne of shrimps.
Make pastry dough for pie and store in a plastic bag in refrigerator.

Morning
Prepare tomatoes for couronne of shrimps; fill mold with aspic, tomatoes and shrimps and store, covered, in refrigerator.
Prepare celery garnish and soak in ice water or wash watercress.
Make the mayonnaise and add juice from the tomato seeds; cut wholewheat bread and keep covered with plastic wrap.
Prepare and bake apple pie.
Prepare new potatoes and peas and keep in cold water ready for cooking.
Roast duck and cut in pieces. Make sauce, spoon over duck in casserole and keep in refrigerator ready for final cooking. Pit olives for garnish.

Assemble ingredients for final cooking from 7 p.m. for dinner around 8 p.m.

Order of Work
7:00
Set oven at moderate (350°F). Unmold couronne of shrimps onto platter, add garnish and chill. Whip the cream for apple pie and chill.
7:15
Put duck in oven.
7:30
Cook peas and potatoes.
Fry croûtes and broil or fry sausages for duck garnish.
7:50
Toss peas and potatoes in butter, transfer to serving dishes and keep warm.
Heat olives for garnish.
7:55
Turn down oven to low, add sausage and olive garnish to duck, cover and keep warm in oven. Add croûtes just before serving.
8:00
Serve appetizer.

You will find that **cooking times** given in the individual recipes for these dishes have sometimes been adapted in the timetable to help you when cooking and serving this menu as a party meal.

Appetizer

Couronne of Shrimps in Aspic

$\frac{3}{4}$ lb cooked, peeled baby shrimps
4 cups cool but still liquid aspic
4 tomatoes, peeled, seeded and cut in quarters, reserving juice from seeds
small bunch of celery or bunch of watercress, washed (for garnish)
$\frac{3}{4}$ cup mayonnaise

Ring mold (1 $\frac{1}{2}$ quart capacity)

Method
Set the ring mold over a pan of ice water. When very cold, add a little cool but still liquid aspic and tilt the mold until the sides and base are coated. Chill until the aspic is firmly set and repeat the coating if necessary.

Arrange the tomato quarters on the aspic, rounded side down, points towards the outside rim of the mold. Spoon enough cool but still liquid aspic over tomatoes to hold them in place; chill mold over a pan of ice water until set. Fill mold alternately with layers of shrimps and cool aspic, letting each layer of aspic set before adding another layer of shrimps and aspic. Cover mold with plastic wrap; chill 2 hours or until firmly set.

Cut celery into julienne strips and let stand in ice water for about 30 minutes until they curl at the ends; drain thoroughly.

To serve: dip the mold into warm water and turn it out onto a platter. Fill center with the celery curls or a bunch of watercress.

Work the juice from the tomato seeds through a strainer, mix with mayonnaise and serve separately. Serve the mold with thinly sliced and buttered wholewheat bread.

Arrange tomato quarters on the layer of chilled aspic, rounded side down

Place a layer of shrimps on tomatoes, pour on a layer of cool aspic and chill

Couronne of shrimps in aspic, garnished with watercress or celery, if you like, makes an attractive appetizer

To Make Aspic

For 4 cups: sprinkle 2 envelopes of gelatin over $\frac{1}{4}$ cup sherry and $\frac{1}{4}$ cup white wine in a small pan and leave 5 minutes or until spongy. Pour $3\frac{1}{2}$ cups cold fish or chicken stock into a scalded pan or kettle and add 1 teaspoon wine vinegar. Whisk 2 egg whites to a froth, add them to pan, set it over moderate heat and whisk backwards and down until the stock is hot. Add gelatin, and continue whisking until mixture boils.

Stop whisking and let liquid rise to the top of the pan; turn off heat or draw pan aside and leave to settle for about 5 minutes. Bring to a boil again, draw pan aside once more and leave liquid to settle. At this point, the liquid seen through the egg white filter should look clear. If not, repeat the boiling process. Strain the aspic through a scalded dish towel or jelly bag; cool before using.

For detailed instructions, see Volume 8.

Couronne means crown in French and couronne of shrimps in aspic refers to the circular shape of the mold.

Entrée

Salmis of Duck with Olives

4–5 lb duck
salt and pepper
2 tablespoons butter
1 shallot, finely chopped
1½ tablespoons flour
2 cups chicken stock
½ cup dry white wine
bouquet garni

For garnish
8–10 chipolata or country sausages
8–10 green olives, pitted
2–3 slices of bread, crusts removed, cut in triangles and fried in 3–4 tablespoons oil and butter, mixed (for croûtes)

Method

Set oven at hot (425°F).

Prick the skin of the duck thoroughly to let fat escape during cooking. Place duck in a roasting pan on a wire rack, sprinkle with seasoning and roast, basting occasionally, in heated oven 1 hour or until the duck is browned and well drained of fat. Remove excess fat from pan during cooking.

Melt the butter in a large saucepan, stir in the shallot and cook gently until just soft. Stir in the flour and cook until browned. Take from the heat and gradually stir in 1 cup of the stock and the wine. Bring to a boil, stirring, season, add bouquet garni and continue simmering for 20 minutes.

Pour ½ cup remaining cold stock into sauce, bring to a boil and skim the surface thoroughly. Add remaining cold stock, bring to a boil and skim again; taste for seasoning and remove the bouquet garni.

Remove duck from the roasting pan, carve it into 4 serving pieces and put the pieces in a casserole. Spoon over the sauce, cover, turn down oven heat to moderate (350°F) and continue baking duck about 30–40 minutes longer or until it is very tender.

To prepare garnish: broil or fry sausages until lightly browned. Soak olives in hot water for 1 minute to heat them.

Remove lid of casserole, garnish duck with sausages and drained olives and arrange fried croûtes around edge of pot. Serve with new potatoes and green peas.

Carve the roast duck into quarters and place them in a casserole ready for baking

After garnishing the dish with the sausages and olives, arrange the croûtes around the salmis

Dessert

Tarte aux Pommes Grillée
(Latticed Apple Pie)

1 cup quantity of rough puff pastry (see Volume 2) or puff pastry (see Volume 8)
4–5 Golden Delicious or other firm dessert apples
6 tablespoons sugar
2 cups water
4 tablespoons apricot jam
confectioners' sugar (for sprinkling)
½ cup heavy cream, whipped until it holds a stiff peak (for serving)

9 inch pie pan

Method

Dissolve the sugar in the water and boil it for 2 minutes. Work apricot jam through a strainer into syrup and stir thoroughly until jam is melted.

Pare, quarter and core apples. Put them in the syrup, cover pan and bring to a boil.

Watchpoint: apples should be completely covered by syrup, so if necessary poach them in 2 batches.

Poach the apples over a low heat for 12–15 minutes, then take pan from the heat and let stand until cold; at the end of this time the apple quarters should look transparent.

Set oven at hot (425°F).

Arrange the apples, cut side down, in the pie pan. Roll out pastry dough, cut and press a broad strip around the rim of the pie pan. Cut 10–12 strips about ½ inch wide from the remaining dough and lay over the apples in a lattice pattern, twisting them if you like. Sprinkle the top with confectioners' sugar and bake in heated oven for 15–20 minutes or until the pastry is brown. Serve the pie cold with whipped cream.

Spoon the poached apple quarters, rounded side up, into the pie pan

Twist the strips of dough and make a lattice pattern over the apples

Salmis is the name given to a brown ragoût of duck or game. The bird is always lightly roasted before it is split or carved and cooked a little longer.

Duck with a difference

Apple pie is decorated with a lattice of pastry before baking; serve cold with whipped cream

English-style muffins (recipe is on page 47) are delicious toasted and spread with butter

BRITISH COOKING

The traditional cooking of Britain is very simple; meats are roasted or stewed, fish is usually fried, vegetables are boiled and there is little tendency as in France to combine many ingredients. Sauces, for example, are rare in British cooking – a little white sauce for vegetables perhaps, gravy with meat, bread sauce with poultry and game – and that is almost as far as it goes. But such simple cooking need not be dull – at its best British food is a superb blend of top quality ingredients that are plainly cooked so that each individual flavor is very clearly defined.

To spice these simple foods, the British add contrasting accompaniments – horseradish cream with beef and mint sauce with lamb. Hot spicy mustard is a favorite condiment and pickles and relishes are an important addition to cold meats, a regular feature of British tables.

The British eat large quantities of baked goods and every region has its traditional specialty, though few cooks still observe the old-fashioned weekly 'baking day'. Chelsea buns – made from a yeast dough rolled with butter and currants – originated in London; a dark oatmeal cake called parkin comes from Yorkshire, and the Welsh make their own buttermilk pancakes. The Scots excel in making all breads and cakes and are famous for their bannocks (flat round cakes sometimes made with a yeast dough, sometimes with a baking powder batter), their oatcakes (crisp wafers made with rolled oats) and their buttery, crumbling shortbread.

As in America, the best cooking is done at home in Britain because the simple recipes often depend on care and exact timing that are hard to achieve in a restaurant.

Regional Specialties

Fish has long been a staple food in Britain. The cold waters of the North Sea are fertile fishing grounds so that cod, haddock, herring, mackerel and whiting are less expensive than all but the cheapest cuts of meat. Luxury fish like Dover sole, turbot and halibut are readily available fresh almost everywhere even if they are expensive. Shellfish is scarce except for the delicious baby shrimps, $\frac{3}{4}$–1 inch long, that are often 'potted' – spiced with mace, pepper, salt and a touch of cayenne, then packed in containers with a layer of butter on top to keep them fresh.

The hunting and fishing rights for the best river fish like salmon and trout, and game such as pheasant, grouse, partridge, snipe, woodcock and duck, are protected by law but supplies in the markets in season are abundant though expensive. The quality of Scotch salmon is renowned and the flesh is rich and close-textured. Scotch smoked salmon is also famous (smoked salmon is so expensive, not because the smoking process is difficult but because the fish loses so much weight during the smoking).

Puddings are popular throughout Britain – hearty, warming dishes are essential in a climate where it is rarely very cold or very hot, but invariably damp. Many of them are named after the towns where they originated – Canterbury pudding is a steamed sponge served with a wine sauce; Cheltenham pudding is baked with dried fruits including ginger and served with hard sauce, and Exeter pudding has a light breadcrumb base, flavored with raisins and blackcurrant jam and enriched with plenty of eggs. The puddings are not all sweet – steak and kidney pudding, made with suet pastry, is a great favorite.

Pies are another British specialty – they are often deep dish pies with a top rather than a bottom crust, but double crust pies are also common. Fruit is the usual filling for sweet pies, and savory pies are made with mixtures varying from seafood to steak and kidney to veal and ham. The famous pork pie, with a solid crisp crust made with lard, is even sold in tiny villages, and every pork butcher has his own secret recipe. Equally individual are the fresh pork sausages known colloquially as 'bangers' from their habit of bursting with a bang when cooked at too high a heat. Skinned 'bangers' are sometimes wrapped in puff pastry to make sausage rolls – a popular lunch time snack that is available, with pork pie, in pubs with a pint of draft beer.

Typical British beer is rich and dark with little effervescence and it is always served, to the bewilderment of Americans, at room temperature (50°F–60°F). In the Southwest of England hard cider vies with beer as the local drink – this cider also is almost without bubbles and it is left to ferment until little sugar remains, so the alcoholic content is sometimes higher than beer.

Welsh Granny's Broth

3 lb neck of mutton or lamb
4–5 leeks
$2\frac{1}{2}$ quarts cold water
salt and pepper
$\frac{3}{4}$ lb carrots, halved
1 small yellow turnip or rutabaga, sliced
4 medium potatoes, quartered
1 tablespoon flour (mixed to a paste with $\frac{1}{4}$ cup cold water)
3 tablespoons chopped parsley

Traditionally the broth from this recipe is served as the appetizer of a meal with the meat and vegetables as the entrée. This and the following soup recipe use the once ubiquitous mutton of the hill areas of Britain.

Method

Trim the leeks, split them almost to the root and wash well. Cut off the green tops, reserve and slice leeks finely.

Trim any fat from the meat and put the meat in a kettle. Cover with cold water, add seasoning, bring slowly to a boil and skim carefully. Add carrot, turnip or rutabaga, and white part of the leeks. Cover and simmer 2–$2\frac{1}{2}$ hours or until the meat is almost tender.

Add potatoes and continue to simmer 30 minutes or until vegetables and meat are very tender. Stir flour paste into hot soup to thicken it. Add green part of leeks and the parsley and simmer 10 minutes longer.

Adjust seasoning and serve broth first and meat and vegetables as a separate course or serve all together in large bowls.

Scotch Broth

$1\frac{1}{2}$ lb neck of mutton or lamb
2 quarts water
salt and pepper
2 tablespoons pearl barley
2 medium white turnips, diced
1 large carrot, diced
1 large onion, diced
1 tablespoon chopped parsley

Method

Trim any fat from the meat and put the meat in a kettle with the water. Season, bring slowly to a boil, and skim carefully. Cover and simmer 1 hour.

Add the barley and simmer 1 hour longer. Add the vegetables and continue cooking 45 minutes or until vegetables and meat are very tender.

Lift out meat, cut it from the bone and dice it; return to soup, reheat, taste for seasoning and serve with chopped parsley sprinkled on each bowl.

Scotch broth is a homey satisfying soup

Salmon with Piquant White Sauce

4 salmon steaks, cut $\frac{3}{4}$–1 inch thick
$\frac{1}{4}$ cup butter
salt and pepper

For piquant white sauce
$1\frac{1}{2}$ teaspoons sugar
1 teaspoon dry mustard
1 tablespoon oil
2 egg yolks
2 tablespoons white wine vinegar or tarragon vinegar
$\frac{3}{4}$ cup milk
$\frac{1}{4}$ cup heavy cream

To serve
3 cups shelled fresh green peas
sprig of fresh mint
1 teaspoon butter
1 teaspoon sugar

Method

To make piquant white sauce: mix sugar, mustard and a little salt in the top of a double boiler and stir in the oil. Stir in egg yolks, then the vinegar. Pour in milk and heat mixture, stirring constantly with a wooden spoon, over hot but not boiling water for 8–12 minutes or until sauce thickens enough to coat the back of the spoon. Add more salt to taste and keep warm in double boiler.

Watchpoint: do not let sauce become too hot or it will curdle.

In a skillet heat the $\frac{1}{4}$ cup butter, sprinkle salmon steaks lightly with seasoning on both sides, sauté for about 5 minutes on each side or until lightly browned and fish flakes easily when tested with a fork.

Arrange the salmon steaks down one side of a hot platter and keep warm.

Cook peas in boiling salted water with the mint for about 10 minutes or until just tender, then drain, refresh and toss with the butter and sugar. Pile peas down the other side of the platter. Stir cream into sauce and serve separately.

Roast Pike

4–$4\frac{1}{2}$ lb whole pike, cleaned and head removed
$\frac{1}{2}$ cup butter
1 cup ale
1 cup water

For stuffing
2 onions, finely chopped
$\frac{1}{4}$ cup butter
$1\frac{1}{4}$ cups fresh white breadcrumbs
$\frac{1}{4}$ cup chopped parsley
1 tablespoon chopped mixed herbs (thyme, rosemary, sage)
grated rind and juice of 1 1 lemon
6 anchovy fillets, crushed, or 1 tablespoon anchovy paste
1–2 eggs, beaten to mix
pepper
salt (optional)

Trussing needle and string or poultry pins

This recipe comes from the Lake District of Cumberland. Bass or almost any other white fish can be substituted for the pike and, if you prefer, use red or white wine instead of ale.

Method

Set oven at moderate (350°F). Wash fish well, scraping off scales, if necessary, and dry it.

To make stuffing: cook onion in the butter until soft; stir in the breadcrumbs, herbs, lemon rind and juice and anchovy fillets or paste. Add enough egg to bind the stuffing so it is moist but not wet and season well with pepper and a pinch of salt, if you like.

Stuff the pike with the mixture and sew it up with string or fasten with poultry pins. Set the pike in a buttered baking dish, spread it with the butter and pour over the ale and water. Cover the dish with buttered foil, pressing it well down over the fish and bake in the heated oven for 20 minutes.

Increase oven heat to moderately hot (375°F), remove the foil and bake for 15–25 minutes longer, or until the fish flakes easily when tested with a fork and the skin is brown and crisp. Baste often during cooking as pike tends to be dry.

Pour pan juices over each serving of fish and serve a savory butter, such as tomato or anchovy butter, separately.

Anchovy Butter

Cream 3–4 tablespoons butter. Crush or pound the 4 anchovy fillets (soaked in milk to remove excess salt) and work in butter with black pepper and enough anchovy paste to accent the flavor and color. Roll into a cylinder the diameter of a quarter on wax paper and chill. Cut into circles.

Tomato Butter

Substitute $1\frac{1}{2}$ teaspoons tomato paste and 3–4 drops Worcestershire sauce with salt and pepper for anchovies and paste in above recipe.

Steak with Oyster Sauce

4 fillet or strip steaks, cut $\frac{3}{4}$–1 inch thick
1 tablespoon oil
$\frac{1}{4}$ cup port
bunch of watercress (for garnish)

For oyster sauce
$\frac{1}{2}$ pint oysters with their liquor
1 cup beef stock
1 teaspoon arrowroot (mixed to a paste with 1 tablespoon water)
salt and pepper

Before the beginning of this century oysters were inexpensive in England and they were often combined with meat.

Method

In a heavy skillet heat the oil and fry the steaks over high heat until well browned, allowing 3 minutes on each side for rare fillet steak, and 4 minutes for rare strip steak. Add port, then heat and flame. Take steaks from pan, arrange on a hot platter and keep warm.

To make oyster sauce: add beef stock to the pan and bring to a boil, stirring, to dissolve the pan juices. Add the oysters with a little of their liquor and cook just until the edges curl. Stir in arrowroot paste and cook gently until the sauce thickens.

Taste sauce for seasoning, spoon over the steaks, garnish with watercress and serve boiled small new potatoes separately.

Mince

2 lb lean ground beef
2 tablespoons beef drippings or oil
1 large onion, finely chopped
2 tablespoons flour
1½–2 cups stock or water
salt and pepper
2 slices of bread, crusts removed (for garnish)

If the British have an equivalent of hamburger, it is mince – a smooth mixture of ground beef in gravy that is usually served with sippets and mashed potatoes or boiled rice. Mince must be cooked very slowly so the consistency is creamy and the color is a rich brown.

Method

In a skillet heat beef drippings or oil, add onion and cook until soft. Add ground beef and cook over brisk heat, stirring constantly to break up the meat, until it is well browned. Stir in the flour, add 1½ cups stock or water and seasoning, bring to a boil, cover and simmer very gently for 1½–2 hours or until the meat is tender and the mixture is creamy and fairly thick. Add a little more liquid during cooking if the mixture looks dry and stir occasionally.

To serve, toast bread and cut each slice of hot toast into 8 small triangles (sippets). Transfer the mince to a hot platter; scatter sippets on top or arrange them around the edge.

Cornish pasty is filled with steak and a variety of vegetables – onion, potato, carrot and turnip

Cornish Pasties

These pasties and variations called 'clangers', filled with meat and vegetables, are made throughout England. Originally they were eaten by miners working in the tin mines; meat was put at one end of the pasty (a pastry shell shaped like an inverted boat) and apple at the other, so the pasty made a complete meal that was easy to carry.

Good Cornish pasties are made with top quality steak and all the good flavor and juices of the meat are kept inside the pastry. Added vegetables vary – some cooks include carrot, for instance, others do not.

Cornish Pasties

For drippings pastry
2 cups flour
pinch of salt
6 tablespoons beef drippings, chilled, or lard
about 5 tablespoons cold water

For filling
½–¾ lb sirloin, strip or other top quality steak
1 large onion, chopped
2 medium potatoes, diced
1 carrot, diced
1 small turnip, diced
salt and pepper

Makes 4–5 individual pasties or 1 large one.

Method

To make drippings pastry dough: sift flour with salt. Add chilled drippings or lard and rub in with the fingertips or cut in with a knife until the mixture resembles crumbs. Stir in enough cold water to make a firm dough and work until smooth. Chill 30 minutes.

Set oven at hot (400°F). Cut steak in very small pieces and combine with vegetables and plenty of seasoning.

Roll out dough about ¼ inch thick and cut into 4–5 six inch circles or 1 large circle. Pile filling in center of each dough circle and brush edges with water. Bring opposite edges together over top of filling, pinch together to seal. Flute to form a ridge along the tops, and curve ends of pasties down to a crescent shape. Set the pasties or pasty on a baking sheet and bake in heated oven for 20–25 minutes or until browned.

Cover with foil – for a large pasty, tuck down foil at sides; lower oven heat to moderate (350°F) and bake 30–35 minutes for small pasties or 1 hour for a large one to cook meat. Serve hot or cold.

Steak and kidney pudding is steamed in a beef suet pastry and traditionally served with a napkin tied around the bowl

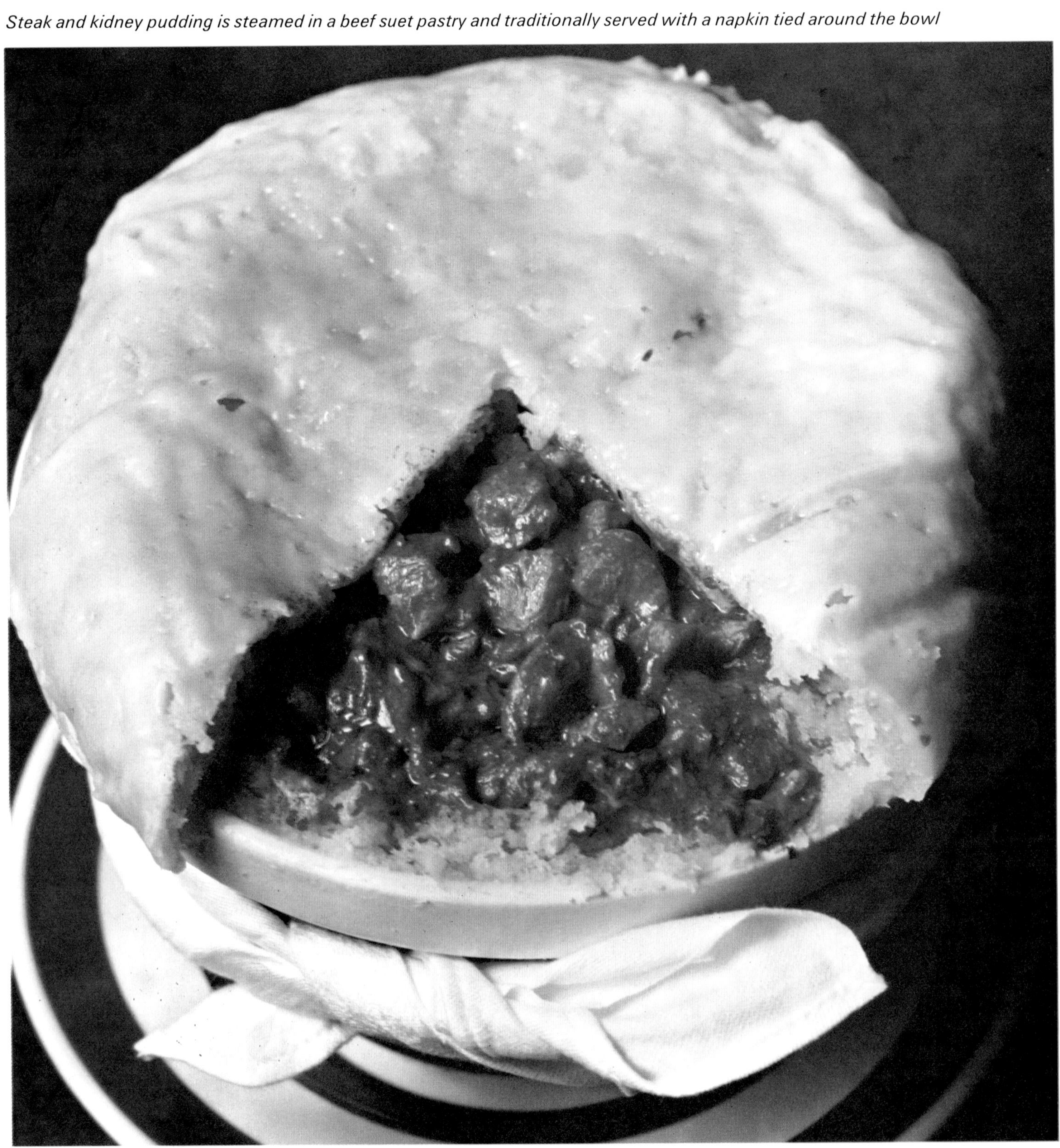

Steak and Kidney Pudding

$1\frac{1}{2}$ lb chuck or round steak, cut in $\frac{1}{2}$ inch cubes
$\frac{1}{2}$ lb beef kidney, cut in $\frac{1}{2}$ inch cubes
1 small onion, chopped
2 teaspoons chopped mixed herbs (parsley, thyme, oregano)
2 tablespoons flour
salt and pepper
1 cup water

For suet pastry
2 cups self-rising flour
pinch of salt
$\frac{1}{2}$ cup ground beef suet
$\frac{3}{4}$ cup water

Heatproof bowl ($1\frac{1}{2}$ quart capacity)

Method

To make suet pastry dough: sift the flour into a bowl with a pinch of salt. Stir in the suet, then stir in enough water to make a dough that is soft but not sticky. Turn onto a floured board and knead lightly until pliable. Use at once.

Grease the bowl. Roll out two-thirds of the pastry (reserving the other third to make the lid) to a round about 1 inch thick, sprinkle with flour and fold in half. To mold the folded pastry to fit the bowl, with hands pull ends of folded edge to make a pocket the shape of bowl. Roll folded dough lightly until it is $1-1\frac{1}{2}$ inches thick (each layer will be $\frac{1}{2}-\frac{3}{4}$ inch thick) and line the bowl with it.

Mix the steak, kidney, onion, herbs, flour and seasoning together thoroughly and pile into the dough-lined bowl. Pour in water. Roll out rest of dough to cover top of bowl, lay it on top of meat mixture and press the edges of dough together to seal, then trim them.

Scald a clean cloth and sprinkle the surface with flour. Make a 1 inch pleat in the center to allow for rising and lay it over the pudding, floured side down. Tie a string around the cloth and bowl, then lift up the 4 corners of the cloth and tie them together on top of the bowl, so it is easy to lift.

Put the bowl in a kettle of boiling water to cover, add the lid, and boil steadily for 3–4 hours, filling the pan with more hot water as necessary to keep the pudding covered.

To serve, take off cloth and tie a clean, folded white napkin around bowl. Serve with a small pitcher of boiling water. Cut the first portion in a wedge and pour in a little water to increase and dilute the rich gravy.

For steak and kidney pudding, carefully lift suet pastry dough 'pocket' to line the bowl

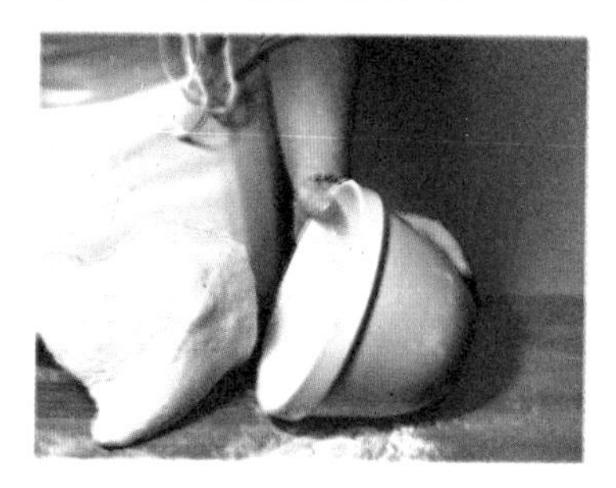

Leek Pie

2 cup quantity of pie pastry (see Volume 1)
5–6 medium leeks
2 tablespoons butter
salt and pepper
2 slices of bacon, finely diced
1 egg, beaten to mix with $\frac{1}{2}$ teaspoon salt (for glaze)

For custard
1 egg
1 egg yolk
1 cup milk, scalded

9 inch pie pan

Method

Make pie pastry dough and chill 30 minutes. Set oven at moderately hot (375°F).

Trim the leeks, halve them lengthwise and wash them well; slice finely. In a saucepan melt butter, add leeks and seasoning, press a piece of foil on top, add lid and sweat (cook very gently) for 10–12 minutes or until leeks are very tender. Fry the bacon until beginning to brown (but not crisp) and drain on paper towels.

Roll out half the dough, line into pie pan, prick bottom of dough with a fork and brush edge with water. Mix leeks with bacon and plenty of pepper and spread mixture in the pie shell. Roll out remaining dough into a 9 inch circle, lay it on top of pie and press the edges to seal them. Flute or scallop edges, if you like, and make a hole in center of pie. Brush with egg glaze and bake in heated oven for 25–30 minutes or until the pastry is firm.

To make custard: beat the egg and egg yolk until mixed and gradually stir in the scalded milk.

Pour the custard into the pie through the hole and continue baking 12–15 minutes or until a skewer inserted through hole comes out clean and pastry is brown. Serve hot or cold.

Cottage Pie (Shepherd's Pie)

mince made with 2 lb ground beef (see recipe for mince on page 39)
1 tablespoon butter
16–18 small onions, blanched and peeled
2 teaspoons sugar
salt and pepper (for topping)
mashed potatoes (made with 3 medium potatoes, $\frac{3}{4}$ cup hot milk, $1\frac{1}{2}$ tablespoons butter)

Ovenproof dish (2 quart capacity)

Method

In a shallow saucepan or skillet heat the butter, add the onions and sprinkle with sugar and a little salt. Sauté gently, shaking the pan occasionally, until the sugar caramelizes and the onions are well coated and brown. If onions are not tender by the time the sugar has caramelized, cover pan and continue cooking over low heat until they are done.

Spread half the mince in the dish, arrange onions on top and add remaining mince. Season mashed potato, cover pie with it and roughen the surface with a fork. Bake pie in a moderate oven (350°F) for 25–35 minutes or until top is browned and meat gravy begins to bubble up around the edge of the potatoes.

Note: cottage pie can be made a day ahead and stored in refrigerator. Dot surface of potato with a little butter or drippings before reheating.

Fidget Pie

1 cup quantity of rough puff pastry (see Volume 2)
1 cup cooked ham, cut in strips, or 8 slices of bacon, finely diced
4–5 medium potatoes, thickly sliced
3 onions, thinly sliced
3 tart apples, pared, cored and sliced
1 tablespoon sugar
salt and pepper
about 1½ cups stock
1 egg, beaten with ½ teaspoon salt (for glaze)

9–10 inch deep oval or round pie dish

This Shropshire pie used to be made at harvest time.

Method
Make the pastry dough and chill 30 minutes.

Set oven at hot (400°F).

Butter the pie dish and arrange the ham or bacon, potatoes, onions and apples in layers in pie dish, sprinkling each layer with a little of the sugar and salt and plenty of pepper. Pour over the stock.

Roll out two-thirds of the dough to cover the pie dish. Roll remaining dough into a long strip, cut it into strips ¾ inch wide and set a strip of dough around the edge of the pie dish. Press down well and brush with water. Lift the large piece of dough and lay it carefully over the dish. Trim, then scallop or flute the edges of the pie (see Volume 1). Make a hole in the center of pie to allow steam to escape. Brush pie with egg glaze. Twist the remaining strips of dough and arrange them on the pie as decoration; brush them also with egg glaze. Bake pie in heated oven for 30 minutes or until pastry is well browned.

Wrap a piece of foil over the pie and tuck down well at the sides. Turn down oven heat to moderate (350°F) and bake 30–40 minutes longer or until the vegetables are tender when the pie is pierced with a skewer. Serve hot with buttered cabbage or cold without an accompaniment.

Apple and Onion Pie

1½ cup quantity of rich pie pastry (see Volume 1)
3 medium tart apples, pared, cored and sliced
2 onions, sliced, blanched and drained
1 teaspoon sage
salt and pepper
pinch of allspice
¼ cup clotted cream (see box)

8 inch flan ring or 9 inch pie pan with removable base

This Cornish dish can be eaten with cold meat or cheese; 3 tablespoons heavy cream or 2 tablespoons butter can be substituted for clotted cream.

Method
Make pie pastry dough and chill 30 minutes.

Set oven at hot (400°F). Roll out half the pastry and line flan ring or pie pan. Brush edge with water and prick bottom of dough with a fork. Arrange half the apples in pie shell, scatter over blanched onion and sprinkle with sage, seasoning, and allspice. Cover with remaining apples; spread clotted cream on top.

Roll out remaining dough to cover pie, lay it on top, trim edges, seal them and flute or scallop with the finger and thumb. Make a hole in center for steam to escape. Bake in heated oven 35–40 minutes or until pastry is browned and apples are tender. Cool slightly, then remove flan ring or pie pan ring. Serve warm.

Fidget pie, a traditional Shropshire pie, used to be made specially at harvest time

Clotted Cream

To make this specialty of the West of England, whole unhomogenized milk is gently heated without boiling for 6–8 hours, then left to cool as slowly as possible. Thick yellow sweet cream, almost as thick as butter, rises to the surface and is skimmed to serve with fruit pies, or instead of butter with hot fresh biscuits and homemade jam.

Stargazy Pie

6 medium herrings
2 cup quantity of pie pastry (see Volume 1) or drippings pastry (see Cornish pasties, page 39)
1 small onion, finely chopped
2 hard-cooked eggs, chopped
1 tablespoon chopped parsley
1½ teaspoons mixed herbs – chervil, dill, thyme
salt and pepper
1 egg, beaten to mix with ½ teaspoon salt (for glaze)

10 inch deep pie pan

Stargazy pie is named because of the fish heads protruding from the pie crust. The idea developed because it was regarded as wasteful to cover inedible fish heads with pastry. However, it was equally wasteful to discard fish heads containing rich oil, so stargazy pie was invented.

There are many different designs and in Cornwall, where the pie originated, it is made with pilchards, a type of giant sardine. Here mackerel may be substituted for the herrings.

Method

Make the pastry dough and chill it 30 minutes. Set the oven at hot (400°F).

With a sharp knife, slit along the backbones of the fish, then continue to cut the flesh away from the bone, using short sharp strokes of the knife, until the bone is detached from the flesh on each side of the fish. Discard the backbones, leaving the fish head holding the fish fillets together, and discard the tail.

Roll out half the dough to a thin round, line the pie dish with it and brush the edge with water. Arrange the herrings on top of the dough with the heads in the center pointing up.

Sprinkle the onion, hard-cooked eggs and herbs over the bodies of the fish and season well.

Roll out the remaining dough to a 10 inch round and cover the pie; press the edges together to seal them and trim. Make a hole in the center and gently pull the heads of the fish through the hole.

Scallop the edge of the pastry (see Volume 1) and brush with egg glaze. Bake in heated oven for 15–20 minutes or until the pastry is browned.

Watchpoint: set pie dish on a hot baking sheet in oven so the lower layer of pastry bakes quickly. When pastry is well browned, lower heat to moderate (350°F) and bake 10 minutes longer.

Cumberland Mutton Pies

1–1$\frac{1}{4}$ lb mutton or lamb, cut from top of leg or shoulder, diced
2 cup quantity of simple raised pie pastry
1 large onion, chopped
1 large carrot, chopped
$\frac{1}{2}$ bay leaf
salt
black pepper, freshly ground
1 egg, beaten to mix with $\frac{1}{2}$ teaspoon salt (for glaze)

8–10 muffin pans; 4 and 3 inch cookie cutters

Makes 8–10 pies.

Method

Put the meat in a pan with the onion, carrot, bay leaf a little salt and plenty of pepper. Add enough water almost to cover, add the lid and simmer 50 minutes or until the meat is very tender. Take from the heat, remove bay leaf and let cool.

Make the pastry dough and chill 2 hours.

Set oven at hot (400°F).

Roll out two-thirds of the dough, cut out 8–10 four inch rounds. Line the rounds into the muffin pans and fill with the meat mixture and a very little of the meat liquid, reserving the remaining liquid.

Roll out the remaining dough, cut out 8–10 three inch rounds and cover the tops of the pies. Pinch the edges together to seal them and flute them between the finger and thumb, if you like.

Make a hole in the center of each pie. Brush the tops with egg glaze and bake in heated oven for 25–30 minutes or until the pastry is well browned.

Heat the remaining meat liquid and pour it into the pies through the hole in the lids while they are still hot. Serve the pies hot or cold.

Simple Raised Pie Pastry

2 cups flour
$\frac{1}{2}$ teaspoon salt
$\frac{1}{2}$ cup softened butter or $\frac{1}{4}$ cup butter and $\frac{1}{4}$ cup shortening
1 small egg, beaten to mix
2–3 tablespoons cold water

Method

Sift the flour and salt onto a board or marble slab. Make a large well in the center and add the butter and shortening, if used, the egg and 2 tablespoons of the water.

Work the ingredients together with the fingertips until the mixture is smooth, then gradually draw in the flour to form a dough, using the whole hand. Add the remaining tablespoon water, if necessary.

Knead the dough lightly until it is smooth, then chill 2 hours or longer before using.

Raised pies are deep two-crust pies, often filled with a savory rather than a sweet mixture. Some are 'raised' by baking in a mold, as here, but others are made with a special pastry using hot water so the pastry is warm and pliable and can be shaped and 'raised' as it cools, like potters clay.

Potted Meats

In the days before refrigeration, one way to preserve meat was to grind or chop it, then pack it, cooked, with seasoning in a sealed crock. The seal and seasonings prevented bacteria from developing and the meat could be kept for several months in a cool place if the seal was unbroken. The most common seal was melted butter or fat.

Salmon and all kinds of game were also potted and these were often taken on long sea voyages to vary the monotonous diet of ship's biscuits and salt meat.

Today potted meats are served as the British equivalent of the French pâtés and terrines. They can be kept, unopened, for up to 2 weeks in the refrigerator, providing they are packed as tightly as possible without liquid (to exclude all air beneath the seal) and then securely sealed.

Potted Ham and Beef

$\frac{3}{4}$ lb chuck or round of beef, cubed
$\frac{3}{4}$ lb country ham, cubed
$\frac{1}{2}$ teaspoon ground allspice
$\frac{1}{4}$ teaspoon ground nutmeg
1 bay leaf
$\frac{1}{2}$ cup water
black pepper, freshly ground
salt (optional)
luting paste (made with 3–4 tablespoons water and $\frac{1}{2}$ cup flour)
$\frac{1}{4}$ cup melted butter (for sealing)

Terrine or casserole (1 quart capacity); bowl (1 quart capacity) or 4 individual ramekins

Method

Put beef and ham with spices, bay leaf and water in the terrine or casserole. Add pepper but do not add salt if the ham is salty. Put on the lid and seal the edge with luting paste made by stirring the water into the flour just until a rough paste is formed.

Set the terrine or casserole in a water bath and bake in a low oven (300°F) for 3 hours. Cool a little, break the seal and remove the bay leaf. Pound mixture until smooth or work it through the fine blade of a grinder.

Season with more spices, if necessary, add salt and pepper to taste and pack it in a bowl or ramekins. Spoon melted butter over the top to seal and chill.

This will keep in refrigerator, covered, for up to 2 weeks.

Potted Tongue

1 lb cooked pickled or smoked beef tongue
1 lb butter, clarified
½ teaspoon ground mace
black pepper, freshly ground (to taste)

Crock or terrine (1 quart capacity)

Method

Chop the tongue and purée half of it in a blender with one-third of the butter. Transfer the mixture to a bowl, purée the remaining tongue with another third of the butter and beat all the tongue purée together with the mace and plenty of black pepper until well mixed.

Pack the mixture into the crock or terrine, making sure all air is excluded. Melt the remaining clarified butter and pour over the top to seal it. Store in the refrigerator and serve chilled with wholewheat bread.

Savories

The British often serve a light savory course after dessert at formal dinners and even at some informal ones. This is usually simple, like sautéed mushrooms, sardines or herring roes on toast, and the 3 following recipes. Sometimes the dish is more elaborate like individual cheese soufflés.

No matter what is served, a savory is usually hot and invariably piquant so it is not overwhelmed by comparison with courses already served. Most savories make excellent cocktail hors d'oeuvre.

Spiced Shrimps

1 cup (½ lb) baby shrimps or medium shrimps, cooked, peeled and chopped
béchamel sauce, made with 2 tablespoons butter, 2 tablespoons flour, 1 cup milk (infused with slice of onion, 6 peppercorns, blade of mace, bay leaf and pinch of cayenne)
½ teaspoon curry powder
salt and pepper
4 slices of bread, crusts removed and fried in 3–4 tablespoons butter or toasted (optional)
2 tablespoons grated Parmesan cheese

4 individual flameproof dishes or ramekins (optional)

Method

Make the béchamel sauce and let cool. Stir in the shrimps, add curry powder and taste for seasoning.

Spread the shrimp mixture on the fried bread or toast or spoon it into the ramekins or dishes. Sprinkle with cheese and broil until browned.

Anchovy and Chicken Liver Toasts

1–2 anchovy fillets, soaked in a little milk and drained
½ cup (¼ lb) chicken livers
2 tablespoons butter
1–2 tablespoons stock
¼ teaspoon paprika
black pepper, freshly ground
4 slices of bread, toasted and crusts removed
2 tablespoons grated Parmesan cheese
2 tablespoons browned breadcrumbs
2 tablespoons melted butter (to finish)

Method

In a frying pan melt the butter and fry the chicken livers for 4–5 minutes or until well browned. Take out and chop them as finely as possible with the drained anchovy fillets. Stir in the stock and paprika with pepper to taste.

Spread the mixture on the toasted bread and cut in fingers. Sprinkle them with a mixture of Parmesan cheese and breadcrumbs and spoon over the melted butter. Bake the toasts in a hot oven (400°F) for 3–4 minutes just before serving.

Mushrooms with Brandy Butter

16 medium mushrooms, stems removed
4 slices of bread, crusts removed

For savory brandy butter
5 tablespoons butter
1 clove of garlic, crushed
1 shallot, finely chopped
2 teaspoons finely chopped parsley
1 tablespoon brandy
salt and pepper

Method

To make brandy butter: cream the butter and mix in the garlic, shallot, parsley and brandy with seasoning.

Place 1 teaspoon brandy butter in each mushroom cap, place them on a baking sheet and bake in a moderate oven (350°F) for 10–12 minutes or until just tender.

Toast bread and cut slices in half, set 2 mushrooms on each piece of bread and serve.

Seed Cake

2 teaspoons caraway seeds
2 cups flour
$\frac{1}{2}$ teaspoon ground nutmeg
1 cup butter
1 cup sugar
5 eggs, separated
$\frac{1}{2}$ cup chopped candied orange peel
3 tablespoons brandy
6–8 cubes of sugar, crushed (for topping)

8 inch springform pan

This is an old-fashioned favorite with afternoon tea.

Method

Grease and flour the cake pan, discarding the excess; set the oven at moderate (350°F).

Sift the flour with the ground nutmeg. Cream the butter, gradually beat in the sugar and continue beating until the mixture is soft and light. Beat the egg yolks, one by one, into the mixture, beating in a teaspoonful of the flour after each one. Stir in the candied peel and caraway seeds.

Stiffly whip the egg whites and fold into the caraway mixture alternately with the remaining flour in 3 batches. Lastly, fold in the brandy.

Transfer the mixture to the prepared pan, sprinkle the top with crushed sugar, and bake in the heated oven for $1\frac{1}{4}$ hours or until a skewer inserted in the center comes out clean. Let cool to tepid in the pan, then transfer the cake to a wire rack to cool completely.

Revel Buns (Saffron Buns)

3 cups self-rising flour
pinch of salt
$\frac{1}{2}$ teaspoon ground cinnamon
$\frac{1}{2}$ cup butter
$\frac{1}{3}$ cup currants
6 tablespoons sugar
$\frac{1}{4}$ cup clotted cream (see box, page 43)
1 egg, beaten to mix
large pinch of saffron, soaked in 2 tablespoons hot milk for 30 minutes and strained
12 sugar cubes, crushed (for sprinkling)

Devonshire Revel buns, flavored with saffron, are made with clotted cream. In this recipe, sour cream may be substituted. Makes 26 buns.

Method

Set oven at moderately hot (375°F); grease baking sheet.

Sift the flour with the salt and cinnamon into a bowl. Rub in the butter with the fingertips until it resembles crumbs, then stir in the currants and sugar. Make a well in center and add cream, egg and flavored milk. Mix with a fork to a fairly firm consistency.

Put mixture 1 tablespoon at a time on the prepared baking sheet, sprinkle buns with crushed sugar and bake in heated oven for 15–20 minutes or until risen and brown.

Welsh Cakes

2 cups self-rising flour
$\frac{1}{3}$ cup butter
pinch of salt
$\frac{1}{2}$ cup currants
$\frac{1}{3}$ cup sugar
1 egg, beaten to mix
3–4 tablespoons milk
sugar (for sprinkling)

Griddle or heavy skillet

Makes 12 cakes.

Method

Rub the butter into the flour with the fingertips. Stir in salt, currants and sugar and make a well in the center. Add the egg and 3 tablespoons milk and mix to a stiff dough, adding more milk if necessary. Roll out the dough on a floured board to $\frac{1}{4}$ inch thickness and cut into 3–4 inch rounds with a cookie cutter.

Lightly grease the griddle or skillet, heat it, cook the cakes over medium heat for 3–4 minutes or until lightly browned. Turn them to brown the other side.

When cold, sprinkle the cakes with sugar and serve with butter.

Anglesey Speckled Bread

2 cups mixed dried and candied fruits, chopped
1 cup hot tea
1 cup brown or granulated sugar
4 cups self-rising flour
pinch of salt
$\frac{1}{4}$ cup butter
1 egg, well beaten

Large loaf pan (9 X 5 X 3 inches)

This bread from the northwestern tip of Wales keeps well for a month or more in an airtight container and the flavor will mellow.

Method

Pour the hot tea over the fruits and sugar, cover and let stand overnight.

Grease the loaf pan and set oven at moderate (350°F).

Sift flour with salt then rub in fat with the fingertips. Make a well in the center and add the egg, the fruit and sugar mixture and stir until thoroughly mixed. Transfer to prepared pan and bake in heated oven for $1\frac{1}{2}$–$1\frac{3}{4}$ hours or until a toothpick inserted in the center of bread comes out clean.

Cool bread a little in the pan, then transfer to a wire rack to cool completely. Cut in slices and spread with butter to serve with fruit or cheese.

Oatmeal Bread

$1\frac{3}{4}$ cups rolled oats
$2\frac{1}{2}$ cups self-rising flour
$\frac{1}{2}$ teaspoon salt
$\frac{1}{2}$ cup butter
1 tablespoon sugar
1 egg, beaten to mix
$\frac{3}{4}$–1 cup milk

Method

Set oven at hot (400°F).

Work rolled oats in a blender a little at a time, until they resemble coarsely ground wholewheat flour.

Mix flour, rolled oats and salt in a bowl. Rub in butter with the fingertips until the mixture resembles crumbs, add sugar and egg with $\frac{3}{4}$ cup milk and work lightly to a dough, adding a little more milk if necessary – the dough should be soft and slightly sticky.

Turn dough onto a lightly-floured baking sheet and pat

out to a round 1–1½ inches thick. Cut into wedges without separating them completely (traditionally these wedges are called farls). Bake in heated oven for 40–45 minutes or until the bread sounds hollow when tapped. Five minutes before the end of baking, separate the wedges and turn them upside down to dry out slightly. Serve with butter.

Crumpets

6 cups flour
1 teaspoon salt
1½ packages dry or 1½ cakes compressed yeast
4–4½ cups lukewarm milk

4 inch crumpet rings (see box, right); griddle or heavy skillet – optional

Makes 18–24 crumpets.

Method
Grease the crumpet rings.

Sift the flour and salt into a warm bowl and make a well in the center. Sprinkle or crumble the yeast over ½ cup of the lukewarm milk and let stand 5 minutes or until dissolved. Pour into the flour, add 3½ cups more milk and stir the mixture with your hand, adding a little more milk, if necessary, to make a batter that is the same consistency as pancake batter. Beat well with the hand for 5 minutes or until batter is very smooth and elastic. Cover with a damp cloth and let rise in a warm place for 45 minutes or until bubbles start to break through the surface of the batter.

Set oven at moderately hot (375°F), if using.

Beat batter lightly to knock out the air.

To cook crumpets on a griddle: set crumpet rings on a hot greased griddle and pour in the batter to fill them three-eighths to half an inch full. Cook over low to moderate heat for 6–7 minutes or until the bottoms of the crumpets are lightly browned. Remove the rings, turn the crumpets and cook for 3–4 minutes on the other side or until lightly browned also.

To bake crumpets in the oven: set crumpet rings on a greased baking sheet, pour in the batter and bake in heated oven for 20–25 minutes or until the crumpets are risen and lightly browned.

Watchpoint: do not brown the crumpets too much as they must be toasted for serving.

To serve, toast the crumpets on both sides and serve with butter and honey or jam.

To make crumpets, pour the batter into rings before cooking them on the griddle

Crumpets and Muffins

Crumpets look much more like our 'English muffins' but they have a spongy texture and are full of porous holes. They are not split before toasting so that butter spread on top melts into the holes and saturates the crumpets. Muffins in England resemble a flat round bread roll and are not at all like our English muffins.

Both crumpets and muffins can be cooked on a griddle or in a heavy skillet and crumpets can also be baked in the oven. Both are made of the same ingredients but the proportions are different so that crumpet mixture is a batter and muffin mixture is a dough.

Both mixtures are shaped in special rings about 4 inches in diameter. Plain 4 inch cookie cutters can be used instead, or use shallow cans such as 8 oz salmon cans with tops and bottoms cut away. Or shape rings from several thicknesses of foil.

Muffins

6 cups flour
1 teaspoon salt
1½ packages dry or 1½ cakes compressed yeast
2–2½ cups lukewarm milk

4 inch muffin rings; griddle or a heavy skillet

Makes 12 muffins.

Method
Sift flour with salt into a warm bowl and make a well in the center. Sprinkle or crumble yeast over ½ cup of lukewarm milk and let stand 5 minutes or until dissolved. Pour into flour, add 1½ cups more milk; work mixture, adding a little more milk if necessary, to make a dough that is soft but not sticky. Turn out onto a floured board and knead 5 minutes or until smooth and elastic.

Place dough in a warm greased bowl, cover with a damp cloth and let rise in a warm place for ¾–1 hour or until doubled in bulk. Work lightly to knock out air; divide into 12 pieces.

Grease rings, place them on a floured board and pat out dough inside them into rounds. Transfer dough in the rings to a greased griddle or heavy skillet and cook over low to moderate heat for about 6–7 minutes on each side or until muffins are risen and lightly browned.

Watchpoint: do not brown muffins too much as they must be toasted for serving.

Toast muffins until they are brown on each side, then split, using 2 forks, to avoid a flatly-cut surface. Sandwich with butter and let stand in a warm place for 5 minutes so butter melts. Serve with jam or honey.

For muffins, pat the dough into rounds inside rings and cook on griddle or in a heavy skillet until lightly browned

Three British breads and cakes include (from left to right) squares of Yorkshire Parkin, Chelsea buns and singin' hinnie

Yorkshire Parkin

2 cups flour
$\frac{1}{2}$ teaspoon salt
$\frac{1}{2}$ teaspoon baking soda
1 teaspoon ground ginger
$\frac{1}{2}$ teaspoon allspice
$1\frac{1}{2}$ cups rolled oats
$\frac{3}{4}$ cup dark brown sugar
$\frac{1}{2}$ cup butter
$\frac{1}{3}$ cup molasses
$\frac{3}{4}$ cup milk

8 inch square cake pan

Parkin is a hearty, close-textured cake that keeps well; in Yorkshire it is always served with apples or cheese.

Method
Grease the cake pan and line it with wax paper; set the oven at moderate (350°F).

Sift the flour with the salt, baking soda and spices and mix well with the rolled oats and sugar; make a well in the center. Melt the butter with molasses, let cool and pour into the flour with the milk. Stir to a smooth batter, pour into the prepared cake pan and bake in the heated oven for 50 minutes or until a skewer inserted in the center comes out clean. Turn out on a wire rack to cool.

Chelsea Buns

$2\frac{1}{2}$ cups flour
pinch of salt
$\frac{1}{2}$ cup butter
5 tablespoons milk
1 package dry or 1 cake compressed yeast
2 eggs, beaten to mix
$\frac{1}{2}$ cup sugar
$\frac{1}{3}$ cup currants
pinch of allspice

8 inch square cake pan

Makes 9 buns.

Method
Sift the flour with the salt into a warm bowl and make a well in the center. Heat half the butter with the milk until butter melts and cool to lukewarm. Sprinkle or crumble over the yeast and let stand 5 minutes until dissolved. Stir in the eggs with $\frac{1}{4}$ cup sugar and pour into the flour. Work to make a smooth, fairly stiff dough, turn out on a floured board and knead 5 minutes or until smooth and elastic.

Put the dough in a warm greased bowl and cover with a damp cloth. Let rise in a warm place for $1-1\frac{1}{2}$ hours or until doubled in bulk. Work dough lightly in the bowl to knock out the air, cover and let rise again for about 30 minutes.

Set the oven at hot (425°F) and grease the cake pan.

Turn dough onto a floured board and roll it out to an 18 × 6 inch rectangle. Spread remaining butter over two-thirds of the dough, and fold in three so the butter is between each layer of dough. Roll out again to an 18 inch square and sprinkle with 3 tablespoons more sugar, the currants and allspice. Roll up the dough like a jelly roll and cut into 9 slices, each 2 inches thick, and place them close together, cut sides up, in the prepared pan. Cover with a damp cloth and let rise in a warm place for 15–20 minutes or until almost doubled in bulk.

Sprinkle dough with remaining sugar and bake in heated oven for 20–25 minutes or until well browned. Cool the buns on a wire rack and separate them before serving.

Singin' Hinnie

3 cups flour
large pinch of salt
scant $\frac{1}{2}$ teaspoon baking soda
1 teaspoon cream of tartar
6 tablespoons lard
$\frac{3}{4}$ cup currants
about 1 cup milk

Griddle or heavy skillet

Singin' hinnie comes from the Tyne river area of the North of England and is named because it sings (sizzles) as it cooks; 'hinnie' means darling.

Method
Sift the flour, salt, baking soda and cream of tartar into a bowl. Rub in the lard with the fingertips until the mixture resembles crumbs, then add the currants. Stir in enough milk to make a fairly soft dough, turn onto a lightly floured board, divide in half and pat or roll each half out to a round about $\frac{1}{4}$ inch thick.

Heat griddle or skillet, lightly flour it and put on a dough round, patting it down. Cook over low heat for about 5 minutes or until browned, turn over and brown on the other side. Take singin' hinnie from the heat. Cool slightly, split and spread with butter. Serve hot. Cook and serve second hinnie in the same way.

Brown both sides of the singin' hinnie on a griddle

Split the hot singin' hinnie and sandwich with butter to serve

Welsh Pancakes

2 cups self-rising flour
$\frac{1}{3}$ cup sugar
pinch of salt
pinch of ground nutmeg
2 eggs, beaten to mix, or
  $\frac{1}{2}$ cup snow
1$\frac{1}{2}$ cups buttermilk
$\frac{1}{4}$ cup melted butter

Griddle or heavy skillet

Makes about 12 pancakes.

Method

If using snow, chill other ingredients. In a bowl, mix the flour, sugar, salt and nutmeg. Make a well in center and add eggs or snow, buttermilk and cooled melted butter. Stir mixture to form a smooth batter, then beat 5 minutes until frothy. Let stand 15 minutes.

Lightly grease griddle or skillet, heat it and pour on enough batter to form 3–4 inch pancakes. Cook over medium heat until pancake bottoms are browned and tops bubbling, then turn to brown the other side.

Pile pancakes one on top of the other while the rest are cooking. Serve hot with butter and fruit preserves or honey.

Selkirk Bannock

6 cups flour
$\frac{1}{2}$ teaspoon salt
$\frac{1}{2}$ cup butter
1$\frac{1}{2}$ cups golden raisins
$\frac{3}{4}$ cup currants
$\frac{1}{2}$ cup mixed candied peel,
  finely chopped
$\frac{1}{3}$ cup sugar
1 package dry or 1 cake
  compressed yeast
1$\frac{1}{2}$–2 cups lukewarm milk
2 tablespoons milk mixed with
  1 tablespoon sugar
  (for glaze)

Method

Sift the flour with the salt into a warm bowl. Rub in the butter with the fingertips until mixture resembles crumbs, stir in the raisins, currants, candied peel and sugar and make a well in the center. Sprinkle or crumble the yeast over $\frac{1}{2}$ cup lukewarm milk and let stand 5 minutes or until dissolved. Pour into the flour with 1 cup more milk. Mix to a fairly firm dough, adding more milk if necessary, then turn out on a floured board and knead for 5 minutes until the dough is smooth and elastic.

Place the dough in a warm greased bowl, cover with a damp cloth and leave in a warm place to rise for 1–1$\frac{1}{2}$ hours or until doubled in bulk.

Set oven at hot (400°F) and lightly flour a baking sheet.

Turn out dough onto the board, work lightly to knock out the air and shape into a large round 2–2$\frac{1}{2}$ inches thick. Set on prepared baking sheet and leave in a warm place to rise for 25 minutes or until almost doubled in bulk.

Bake in heated oven for 40–45 minutes. Brush the bannock with sweetened milk to glaze and bake 10 minutes longer or until well browned and the bannock sounds hollow when tapped on the top. Transfer the bannock to a wire rack to cool.

To serve, cut bannock in $\frac{1}{4}$ inch slices and spread them with butter.

Shortbread

$\frac{3}{4}$ cup unsalted butter
$\frac{1}{2}$ cup sugar
2 cups flour
sugar (for sprinkling)

Shortbread keeps well in an airtight container for 2–3 weeks. Makes about 20–24 bars or an 11 inch round of shortbread.

Method

Set oven at moderately hot (375°F) and lightly butter a baking sheet.

Cream the butter, gradually beat in the sugar and work until the mixture is soft and light. Stir in the flour as quickly as possible to make a soft dough.

Turn onto the prepared baking sheet and pat out the dough to a round or a rectangle about $\frac{3}{4}$ inch thick. Flute or scallop the edges of the circle with finger and thumb and mark into wedges; mark the rectangle into bars about 1 × 3 inches. Prick the dough well all over with a fork, sprinkle generously with sugar and bake in heated oven for 15–20 minutes or until the shortbread is very lightly browned.

Cool on the baking sheet, then break into wedges or bars.

Cloutie Dumpling

3 cups self-rising flour
1 cup ground or finely chopped
  suet
$\frac{3}{4}$ cup currants
$\frac{3}{4}$ cup golden raisins
$\frac{3}{4}$ cup raisins
1$\frac{1}{2}$ teaspoons ground cinnamon
1$\frac{1}{2}$ teaspoons ground ginger
1$\frac{1}{2}$ teaspoons ground allspice
$\frac{2}{3}$ cup dark brown sugar
$\frac{1}{2}$ teaspoon baking soda
$\frac{1}{2}$ teaspoon cream of tartar
$\frac{1}{2}$ tart apple
$\frac{1}{4}$ cup molasses
1 egg, beaten to mix
about $\frac{3}{4}$ cup milk
sugar (for sprinkling)

This giant dumpling is boiled in a cloth and resembles Christmas plum pudding. In parts of Scotland charms like a thimble, sovereigns and sixpences used to be mixed with the pudding for special occasions.

Method

Mix together the flour, suet, dried fruits, spices, sugar, baking soda and cream of tartar. Grate in the apple and stir thoroughly. Make a well in the center. Mix molasses with egg and add to flour mixture. Stir, adding enough milk to make a soft dough the same consistency as biscuit dough. Wrap in a scalded cloth sprinkled with flour and tie loosely so dumpling can expand.

Have ready a kettle containing enough boiling water to cover the dumpling. Lower dumpling into it, cover pan and boil steadily for 3 hours, adding more hot water as necessary to keep the pudding covered.

Drain dumpling well, untie cloth and set the dumpling on an ovenproof platter. Bake dumpling in moderate oven

(350°F) for 10 minutes to dry surface to a glaze. Sprinkle with sugar and serve with crème à la vanille (vanilla custard sauce) or a hard sauce.

In Scotland any dumpling left over is cut in $\frac{1}{2}$ inch slices and fried with bacon for breakfast or supper.

Cloutie dumpling is served hot with vanilla custard sauce

Wrap the dumpling in a scalded floured cloth and tie loosely so it has room to swell

Scottish oatcakes are served with butter curls; they can be eaten with jam or honey or with savory dishes and cheese

Scottish Oatcakes

3¾ cups rolled oats
½ teaspoon salt
1–2 tablespoons melted lard or bacon drippings
about ¾ cup hot water

The oatcakes will keep in an airtight container for up to 3 weeks. Makes two 7 inch rounds to cut into wedges before baking.

Method
Set oven at moderate (350°F) and lightly grease a baking sheet.

Work rolled oats a little at a time in a blender until the mixture resembles coarsely ground wholewheat flour. Mix rolled oats with the salt and make a well in the center. Pour in the fat and stir to mix, adding enough hot water to make a fairly stiff dough. Divide the dough in two and leave one half in the bowl in a warm place. Roll out the other half on a floured board to a round one-eighth inch thick. Trim the edges to a neat round. Cut the round into wedges and transfer them to the prepared baking sheet.
Watchpoint: work quickly as the dough stiffens and dries as it cools.

Roll out and shape the remaining dough in the same way and bake the oatcakes in the heated oven for 10 minutes or until lightly browned and the edges of the cakes are slightly curled. Transfer to a wire rack to cool.

Quickly roll out Scottish oatcakes mixture on a floured board as it dries fast

Yorkshire Oatcakes

3 cups oatmeal
1 teaspoon salt
½ package dry or ½ cake compressed yeast
2 cups lukewarm water

Griddle or heavy skillet

Like Scottish oatcakes, the main ingredients of these cakes are finely ground oatmeal and water, but a little yeast is also added in this recipe that comes from Northern England.

The batter is cooked on a griddle or in a skillet and, in one town, it used to be the custom to cook the cakes only on one side, then peel them off and hang them up to dry. To serve, the cake was hung before an open fire until crisp. This recipe makes three 7 inch oatcakes.

Method
Work the oatmeal in a blender a little at a time until it resembles coarsely ground wholewheat flour. Mix the oatmeal with the salt and make a well in the center. Sprinkle or crumble the yeast over ½ cup lukewarm water and let stand 5 minutes until it is dissolved. Add the remaining water and stir the mixture gradually into the oatmeal to make a batter as smooth as possible. Cover and let stand in a warm place for 1 hour.

Lightly grease the griddle or skillet, heat it and pour on 1 cup of batter. Cook over moderate heat for 4–5 minutes or until lightly browned. Turn the oatcake over and brown on the other side.

Transfer the cake to a wire rack to cool and cut into wedges before quite cold. Cook the remaining batter in the same way.

Raisin Drippings Cake

1½ cups raisins
¾ cup meat drippings or lard
4 cups flour
½ teaspoon salt
½ cup chopped candied peel
¾ cup sugar
1 tablespoon molasses
1–1¼ cups milk
2 eggs, beaten to mix
1 teaspoon baking soda

8 inch square cake pan

Meat drippings give this traditional English cake a rich, hearty flavor.

Method
Line the base of the pan with wax or silicone paper and grease it and the sides of the pan. Set the oven at moderate (350°F).

Sift the flour with the salt into a bowl and rub in the drippings or lard with the fingertips. Add the raisins, candied peel and sugar and mix well so the fruit is coated. Make a well in the center.

Heat the molasses with one-quarter of the milk until it is dissolved and add to the flour with the eggs. Stir to draw in the flour, adding enough of the remaining milk to make a batter that just drops from a spoon when it is gently shaken.

Dissolve the soda in 1 tablespoon milk and stir into the batter. At once transfer the mixture to the prepared pan and bake in heated oven for 1 hour. Reduce heat to moderately hot (325°F) and bake ½ hour longer or until a skewer or toothpick inserted in the center of the cake comes out clean. Cool the cake in the pan for 30 minutes, then turn it out onto a wire rack to cool completely.

Serve the cake thinly sliced with applesauce or sliced Cheddar cheese, or cut it in squares and sandwich with butter.

Simnel Cake

2½ cups cake flour
large pinch of salt
large pinch of baking soda
1½ cups golden raisins
¾ cup currants
¾ cup candied cherries, halved
¼ cup finely chopped mixed candied peel
1 cup butter
grated rind of 2 lemons
1 cup sugar
4 eggs, separated

For decoration
1 egg, beaten to mix
¼ cup white fondant or glacé icing

For almond paste
2 cups whole blanched almonds, ground
1 cup granulated sugar
1 cup confectioners' sugar, sifted
2 egg yolks
1 egg
juice of 1 lemon
1 teaspoon vanilla
1 teaspoon almond extract
1–2 teaspoons orange flower water (optional)

8 inch springform pan

Method
To make almond paste: put the ground almonds and both sugars in a bowl and mix them well. Beat the egg yolks and whole egg with the lemon juice and flavorings and add to the almond mixture. Pound the mixture with the end of a rolling pin for 2–3 minutes to release some of the oil in the almonds, then knead the mixture with your hand to make a smooth paste, working well to release the oil in the almonds. Store in refrigerator in a plastic bag.

Grease the pan, line the bottom and sides with wax paper and grease again. Set the oven at moderate (350°F).

Sift the flour with the salt and baking soda into a bowl. Mix the dried and candied fruits together and toss them with one-third of the flour until thoroughly coated. Cream butter with lemon rind, gradually add the sugar and continue beating until mixture is soft and light. Beat in egg yolks, one by one, beating well after each addition. Beat egg whites until they hold a stiff peak.

Stir half the remaining sifted flour into the butter and sugar mixture, then stir in the fruit and flour mixture. Stir in remaining flour alternately with the beaten egg whites and spoon half the batter into the prepared pan, spreading it a little way up the sides.

Roll just over one-third of the almond paste into a 7 inch round and place it in the pan on top of the cake batter. Cover with the remaining batter and bake in heated oven for 2 hours.

Reduce oven to low (300°F), cover cake with foil if top is well browned and bake about 30 minutes longer or until a toothpick inserted in the center comes out clean. Cool cake for 15 minutes in pan, then turn it out and place on a baking sheet.

To decorate for Mothering Sunday: divide remaining almond paste in two and shape one half into 15–20 even-sized small balls, rolling them between the palms of your hands. Arrange them around the top edge of the cake (but not too near the edge), brush the balls with beaten egg and tie a piece of foil around the cake to hold the balls in position. Bake the cake in a moderately hot oven (375°F) for 7–10 minutes or until almond balls are lightly browned. Let the cake cool.

Remove foil. Warm fondant or glacé icing and pour it in center of cake. Shape remaining almond paste into fruits, arrange them on icing in center and tie a ribbon around cake.

To decorate for Easter Sunday: roll out a little less than half the remaining almond paste to an 8 inch round. Cut out the center with a 3–4 inch plain cookie cutter, lift the ring onto the cake and press it down firmly. Brush with beaten egg. Shape remaining almond paste into even-sized pear shapes or divide into 11 balls (to represent the loyal Apostles). Place these just touching, around top edge of cake and brush again with beaten egg. Flute or scallop inside edge of the almond paste circle with finger and thumb and tie a piece of foil around cake to keep almond balls in place. Bake cake in a moderately hot oven (375°F) for 7–10 minutes or until balls are lightly browned.

Let cool and remove foil. Fill hole in center of almond paste with melted glacé or fondant icing. Set 1–2 yellow chicks and small sugar or chocolate eggs on top of icing and tie a colored ribbon around cake. If you like, write the word 'Easter' and the date on the white icing, using melted chocolate filled into a paper decorating cone.

Almond Paste Fruits

Use the almond paste left over from the simnel cake for making fruits or, to reproduce the colors of the fruits more accurately, make the marzipan for decorations (see Volume 15) that is very light-colored.

Color small quantities of the almond paste at a time, using only 1–2 drops of food coloring, and shape the different fruits, making the shapes and relative sizes accurate. Using a small, clean paint brush, brush them, where appropriate, with dry cocoa or a very little food coloring to shade 'skin' of fruits and use whole cloves to make stalks and 'eyes'. Let the fruits harden 4–5 hours before putting them on cake.

Simnel Cake was traditionally baked to serve on Mothering Sunday, the Sunday halfway through Lent when children went home to visit their families. However, Mothering Sunday has declined in importance and simnel cake is now usually made to celebrate Easter. Simnel is derived from the Old French 'Simenel' meaning fine flour.

The traditional simnel cake is decorated for Mothering Sunday with balls and fruits of almond paste

Pineapple mousse en surprise is decorated with rosettes of whipped cream and pineapple pieces (recipe is on page 64)

COLD MOUSSES AND SOUFFLES

Cold mousses and soufflés are luxuriously rich and delicate. They make ideal party appetizers or luncheon or light supper dishes and they must be prepared several hours ahead so they can set.

The basic mixture for both mousses and soufflés is similar – the only difference is that soufflés are lightened by the addition of beaten egg whites. Soufflés and molded mousses often need a little gelatin added to be firm but still creamy and to keep their shape. Never use more than the recipe specifies.

Savory mousses are often set in a simple ring mold, cake pan or soufflé dish and garnished with watercress, or there are special lobster-shaped molds for lobster and fish-shaped molds for fish. Savory mixtures don't unmold well from fancy peaked molds but sweet mousses can have more imaginative treatment in melon molds or fancy, fluted ring molds.

All cold soufflés should be served in soufflé dishes. Pour the mixture into a dish with a paper collar so that when set it has the traditional look of a hot soufflé.

The cream added to cold soufflés and mousses should always be lightly whipped so that, when a little is lifted on the whisk or beater, it holds a soft shape or leaves a trail across the cream. This gives mousses and soufflés a light, soft texture.

SAVORY MOUSSES & SOUFFLES

Cold savory mousses and soufflés can be made with fish, meat, poultry, cheese or vegetables. The basic ingredient is chopped, ground or flaked and bound with butter, sauce or mayonnaise.

A savory mousse does not always contain eggs but lightly whipped cream is often added to give a soft, spongy texture. Savory soufflés, however, depend on whipped egg whites for their light airy texture.

To Prepare a Soufflé Dish

Make a collar from a double layer of wax or silicone paper. Use tasteless cooking oil to oil paper lightly on the inside so it peels off easily when the soufflé is set. Wrap this band around the dish, so it extends at least $1\frac{1}{2}$ inches above dish. Attach paper to dish with string.

Lobster Mousse

1 large (about 2 lb) live lobster
1 quart court bouillon (for cooking lobster)
velouté sauce (made with 2 tablespoons butter, 2 tablespoons flour and $1\frac{1}{2}$ cups court bouillon from cooking lobster)
3 hard-cooked eggs
1 envelope gelatin
1 cup mayonnaise
1 teaspoon paprika
salt and pepper
$\frac{1}{2}$ cup heavy cream, whipped until it holds a soft shape

For garnish
5–6 tablespoons mayonnaise
2–3 tablespoons tomato juice
bunch of watercress
body shell of lobster

Soufflé dish or springform pan ($1\frac{1}{2}$–2 quart capacity)

Method

Lightly oil the dish or pan.

Plunge lobster into boiling court bouillon, then simmer for 18 minutes and let cool in liquid. Drain lobster, strain court bouillon and make velouté sauce, reserving $\frac{1}{4}$ cup of remaining court bouillon. Cover sauce and cool.

Split lobster and remove meat from shell, discarding head sac and intestinal tract. Cut tail meat in slices, crack claws, chop meat and reserve soft green tomalley from body. Rub body shell with oil and reserve.

Halve eggs, scoop out yolks and work them through a sieve; chop whites. Sprinkle gelatin over reserved court bouillon and let stand 5 minutes until spongy. Mix velouté sauce with mayonnaise, yolks and whites, tomalley and claw meat.

Dissolve gelatin over pan of hot water, stir into lobster mixture with paprika and season. Chill mixture in refrigerator or over pan of ice water, stirring occasionally, until on point of setting. Fold in cream, adjust seasoning and pour into prepared dish or pan. Cover and chill at least 2 hours or until set.

Shortly before serving, unmold mousse onto platter. Thin mayonnaise with tomato juice to a coating consistency and spoon over mousse. Arrange slices of lobster tail meat on top and garnish dish with watercress and lobster shell.

Smoked Trout or Finnan Haddie Mousse

1 medium smoked trout, or 1 medium fillet Finnan haddie
$\frac{1}{2}$ cup milk and $\frac{1}{2}$ cup water (mixed – to cook Finnan haddie)
béchamel sauce, made with 2 tablespoons butter, 2 tablespoons flour and $1\frac{1}{2}$ cups milk (infused with slice of onion, 6 peppercorns, blade of mace and bay leaf)
salt and pepper
$\frac{3}{4}$ cup mayonnaise
1 envelope gelatin
$\frac{1}{4}$ cup chicken stock or water
2 hard-cooked eggs, chopped
$\frac{1}{2}$ cup heavy cream, whipped until it holds a soft shape

To garnish
2 hard-cooked eggs, sliced
$1\frac{1}{4}$ cups aspic (made with 1 can consommé and $\frac{1}{2}$ envelope gelatin)

Soufflé dish (2 quart capacity)

Method

Make béchamel sauce, season well and cool. If using Finnan haddie cook in milk and water on top of stove or in oven for 5–8 minutes or until fish flakes easily when tested with a fork. Cool, flake trout or haddie, removing all skin and bones; there should be about 1 cup fish. Mix cool béchamel sauce with mayonnaise.

Sprinkle gelatin over stock or water and let stand 5 minutes until spongy. Dissolve over pan of hot water and stir into béchamel sauce mixture. Stir in fish and eggs and chill in refrigerator or stand in bowl over pan of ice water, stirring occasionally, until on point of setting. Fold in cream, taste for seasoning and pour into soufflé dish to fill it about three-quarters full. Cover and chill at least 2 hours or until set.

Arrange slices of hard-cooked egg on top of mousse. Spoon enough cool but still liquid aspic over egg slices just to coat them. Chill until set, then spoon remaining aspic, on top of mousse. Chill until set before serving.

To unmold a creamy mixture: tilt the mold sideways and break the airlock by inserting the point of a knife between the mixture and the mold. Turn the mold in a circle so the mixture loosens all around. Put a plate upside down on top of the mold, quickly invert the mold and plate, holding them together. Shake gently and the mold will slip out onto the plate.

Cold mousses and soufflés

A live lobster and some of the other ingredients used for making lobster mousse

Serve cucumber and cheese mousse with vinaigrette dressing

Cucumber and Cheese Mousse

2 cucumbers, peeled, diced and seeds discarded
$\frac{3}{4}$ cup creamed cottage cheese
1 teaspoon onion juice
salt and pepper
1 envelope gelatin
$\frac{1}{4}$ cup cold water
$\frac{3}{4}$ cup boiling chicken stock, vegetable stock or water
2 tablespoons white wine vinegar
1 tablespoon sugar
pinch of ground mace or coriander
$\frac{3}{4}$ cup heavy cream, whipped until it holds a soft shape

For garnish
bunch of watercress
1 large green pepper, cored, seeded, chopped and blanched
$\frac{3}{4}$ cup vinaigrette dressing

Ring mold (1–1$\frac{1}{4}$ quart capacity)

Method

Lightly oil ring mold.

Sprinkle the cucumber lightly with salt. Press between 2 plates for 30 minutes to draw out the juices (dégorger). Rinse with cold water and drain. Mix cheese with onion juice and seasoning.

Sprinkle gelatin over cold water and let stand 5 minutes until spongy. Pour in boiling stock or water and stir until gelatin is dissolved. Stir into cheese and chill in refrigerator or over a bowl of ice water, stirring occasionally.

Mix cucumber with vinegar, sugar and spice. When cheese mixture is cool and on point of setting, stir in cucumber mixture, then fold in whipped cream. Taste for seasoning and spoon mixture into prepared mold. Cover and chill at least 2 hours or until set.

A short time before serving, unmold mousse onto a platter and fill center with watercress. Stir green pepper into vinaigrette dressing and serve separately with rye or pumpernickel bread and butter.

Ham Mousse

1 cup ($\frac{1}{2}$ lb) cooked lean ham
1$\frac{1}{2}$ cups sauce Madère (see Volume 2)
salt and pepper
$\frac{1}{2}$ envelope gelatin
$\frac{1}{4}$ cup stock
1$\frac{1}{4}$ cups aspic (made with 1 can consommé and $\frac{1}{2}$ envelope gelatin)
few drops of red food coloring (optional)
$\frac{3}{4}$ cup heavy cream, whipped until it holds a soft shape
1 tablespoon chopped truffle, or 1 large mushroom, cooked with a little water and lemon juice and chopped (for decoration)

Soufflé dish (1$\frac{1}{2}$ quart capacity)

Method

Work ham twice through the fine blade of a grinder, then pound in a mortar and pestle and work through a sieve. Add sauce Madère to purée and season well. Or, instead of pounding, purée ground ham in a blender with a little sauce Madère. Add remaining sauce to mixture and season well.

Sprinkle gelatin over stock in a small pan and let stand 5 minutes until spongy. Add $\frac{3}{4}$ cup of aspic and melt over pan of hot water. Stir into ham mixture and add a little red food coloring if you like. Chill in refrigerator or over a bowl of ice water, stirring occasionally, until mixture is on point of setting, then fold in whipped cream. Adjust seasoning and pour into soufflé dish leaving space for aspic decoration. Cover and chill at least 2 hours or until firm.

For decoration: add chopped truffle or mushroom to remaining cool but still liquid aspic and pour over cold mousse. Cover and chill again. Serve mousse with green salad and Cumberland sauce.

Game Mousse

Make as for ham mousse, with cooked squab, pheasant, venison, etc. or mixed leftovers of game.

Tongue Mousse

1 cup ($\frac{1}{2}$ lb) cooked tongue
béchamel sauce, made with 2 tablespoons butter, 2 tablespoons flour and 1$\frac{1}{2}$ cups milk (infused with slice of onion, 6 peppercorns, blade of mace and bay leaf)
salt and pepper
$\frac{1}{2}$ cup ($\frac{1}{4}$ lb) cooked lean ham
$\frac{3}{4}$ cup mayonnaise
1 envelope gelatin
$\frac{1}{4}$ cup stock
1 egg white
$\frac{1}{2}$ cup heavy cream, whipped until it holds a soft shape

For garnish
1 cucumber, peeled, seeded and diced
1 pint cherry tomatoes, peeled
1 cup cooked green beans, cut in $\frac{1}{2}$ inch lengths
8–12 ripe olives, pitted
$\frac{1}{4}$ cup vinaigrette dressing

Soufflé dish (1$\frac{1}{2}$ quart capacity)

Method

Lightly oil soufflé dish. Make béchamel sauce, season well and cool. Work tongue and ham through fine blade of a grinder and beat into cooled béchamel sauce. Alternatively, work the tongue and ham with a little sauce in a blender and then add remaining sauce. Stir in mayonnaise.

Sprinkle gelatin over stock in small pan and let stand 5 minutes until spongy. Dissolve over hot water and stir into tongue mixture. Chill in refrigerator or over pan of ice water, stirring occasionally, until mixture is on point of setting. Stiffly whip egg white. Fold whipped cream into tongue mixture and fold in egg white.

Note: egg white improves the texture of the mousse because tongue is very close-textured.

Taste mousse for seasoning, pour into prepared soufflé dish, cover and chill at least 2 hours or until set.

To prepare garnish: sprinkle cucumber lightly with salt, let stand 30 minutes to draw out juices (dégorger), rinse with cold water and drain. Mix with tomatoes, beans and olives and toss with vinaigrette dressing.

Shortly before serving, unmold mousse onto a platter and spoon garnish around the edge.

Onion Juice

There are 2 ways to extract onion juice:

1 Cut a slice off the onion and work the onion on a juicer, as you would squeeze a lemon.

2 Cut a slice off the onion. Hold the onion over a piece of wax paper and scrape cut side with a sharp paring knife.

Chicken Soufflé

- 1 cup ($\frac{1}{2}$ lb) cooked chicken, finely chopped
- velouté sauce (made with 1$\frac{1}{2}$ tablespoons butter, 1$\frac{1}{2}$ tablespoons flour and 1 cup well-flavored chicken stock)
- 1 envelope gelatin
- $\frac{1}{2}$ cup well-flavored chicken stock or water
- $\frac{1}{2}$ cup mayonnaise
- juice of $\frac{1}{2}$ lemon
- salt and pepper
- 2 egg whites
- $\frac{1}{2}$ cup heavy cream, whipped until it holds a soft shape

For garnish
- 1 medium tomato, peeled and cut in very thin slices
- 1$\frac{1}{2}$ cups aspic (made with 1 can consommé and $\frac{1}{2}$ envelope gelatin)

Soufflé dish (3 cup capacity)

Method

Prepare soufflé dish with a paper collar.

Make velouté sauce and let cool. Beat chicken into the cooled velouté sauce. Sprinkle gelatin over stock or water and let stand 5 minutes until soft. Dissolve over a pan of hot water and stir into the chicken mixture with the mayonnaise. Add lemon juice and season to taste. Chill in the refrigerator or over a pan of ice water, stirring occasionally until mixture is on the point of setting. Stiffly whip the egg whites.

When mixture starts to set, fold in the whipped cream, then the egg whites and pour mixture into the prepared soufflé dish. Chill at least 2 hours or until set.

Arrange slices of tomato on top of the soufflé and spoon over a little of the cool but still liquid aspic to coat them. Chill until set. Spoon remaining cool but still liquid aspic on top of the soufflé; chill thoroughly.

Shortly before serving, carefully remove paper collar. Serve the soufflé with a green salad, if you like.

SWEET MOUSSES & SOUFFLES

A cold sweet mousse is made with whole eggs plus extra egg yolks, beaten together with sugar until thick. Then some kind of flavoring is added (often this is a fruit purée) and the mixture is enriched with whipped cream and lightly set with gelatin.

For a cold sweet soufflé the eggs are always separated; the yolks are beaten with sugar and flavoring (this may be juice or purée) until thick, or made into a custard with milk. Whipped cream is often added and the stiffly whipped egg whites are folded in to give the mixture the characteristic light soufflé texture.

For how to prepare the soufflé dish, see page 58.

Strawberry Mousse

- 1 pint strawberries
- 2 eggs
- 1 egg yolk
- 6 tablespoons sugar
- juice of $\frac{1}{2}$ lemon
- 1 envelope gelatin
- $\frac{3}{4}$ cup heavy cream, whipped until it holds a soft shape

For decoration
- $\frac{1}{2}$ cup heavy cream, stiffly whipped
- 2 tablespoons finely chopped pistachios or browned almonds

Ring or charlotte mold (1 quart capacity); pastry bag and medium star tube

Method

Lightly oil the mold.

Put eggs, egg yolk and sugar in a bowl and beat until mixed. Set the bowl over a pan of hot but not boiling water and beat until the mixture is thick and light and leaves a ribbon trail when the beater is lifted. Take from heat and beat until the mixture is cool. If using an electric beater, no heat is needed. Add enough water to the lemon juice to make $\frac{1}{4}$ cup, sprinkle gelatin over and let stand 5 minutes until spongy.

Hull the strawberries and purée them in a blender or work through a nylon strainer – there should be about 1 cup purée. Dissolve gelatin over a pan of hot water and stir into the egg mixture with the strawberry purée. Chill bowl over pan of ice water, stirring gently until mixture is on the point of setting. Fold in lightly whipped cream and pour at once into the prepared mold; cover and chill at least 2 hours or until set.

Shortly before serving, unmold the mousse onto a platter. Put the stiffly whipped cream into pastry bag fitted with the star tube and decorate the mousse with rosettes of whipped cream; sprinkle them with chopped nuts.

Caramel Mousse

- 3 eggs
- 2 egg yolks
- $\frac{1}{4}$ cup sugar
- juice of 1 lemon
- 1 envelope gelatin
- $\frac{1}{2}$ cup heavy cream, whipped until it holds a soft shape

For caramel
- $\frac{3}{4}$ cup sugar
- $\frac{3}{4}$ cup water

For decoration
- $\frac{1}{2}$ cup heavy cream, stiffly whipped
- fresh strawberries or raspberries (optional)

Fluted or plain ring mold (1 quart capacity); pastry bag and medium star tube

Method

Lightly oil the mold.

To make caramel: heat sugar with half the water in a pan until dissolved, then boil steadily to a rich brown caramel. Take pan from heat, cover hand holding the saucepan with a cloth to avoid splashing and at once carefully add remaining water. Stir until the caramel is melted, heating gently if necessary, and cool.

Put eggs, egg yolks and sugar in a bowl and beat until mixed. Set the bowl over a pan of hot but not boiling water and beat until mixture is thick and light and leaves a ribbon trail when the beater is lifted. Take from heat and beat until cool. If using an electric beater, no heat is needed.

Add enough water to the lemon juice to make $\frac{1}{4}$ cup, sprinkle over gelatin and let stand 5 minutes until spongy. Dissolve gelatin over a pan of hot water and stir into the egg mixture with the caramel. Chill bowl over pan of ice water and stir gently until mixture is on the point of setting. Fold in the lightly whipped cream and pour at once into the prepared mold; cover and chill at least 2 hours or until set.

Shortly before serving, unmold the mousse onto a platter, put the stiffly whipped cream into pastry bag fitted with the star tube and decorate mousse with rosettes of whipped cream. Fill the center with fresh strawberries or raspberries, if you like.

Gelatin: when using gelatin in rich mixtures like soufflés and mousses, the gelatin may separate to the bottom if not stirred until almost set. This applies particularly to the lighter, sweet mousses.

Once gelatin has been added, the mixture should be chilled in a bowl, stirring gently until very cold. At this stage the gelatin will start to set; add the remaining ingredients and pour the mixture into the mold at once because gelatin sets very quickly.

Brown Bread Caramel Mousse with Plum Sauce

4 slices of dry wholewheat bread
$\frac{1}{2}$ cup sugar
2 eggs
1 egg yolk
juice of $\frac{1}{2}$ lemon
1 envelope gelatin
$\frac{3}{4}$ cup heavy cream, whipped until it holds a soft shape

For plum sauce
$\frac{1}{2}$ lb damson or prune plums, pitted
$\frac{1}{4}$ cup sugar or to taste
$1\frac{1}{2}$ cups water

Ring mold (1 quart capacity)

Method

Lightly oil the mold.

Discard the bread crusts and work the bread through a sieve to make crumbs or work it, a slice at a time in a blender. Spread the crumbs on a baking sheet, sprinkle them with 2–3 tablespoons of the sugar and bake in a moderate oven (350°F) for 10 minutes or until they are very crisp and brown with caramelized sugar.

Watchpoint: to brown the crumbs as evenly as possible, turn them often with a fork – the time needed will depend on the freshness of the bread. Let cool to room temperature.

Put the eggs, egg yolk and remaining sugar in a bowl and beat until mixed. Set the bowl over a pan of hot but not boiling water and beat until the mixture is thick and light and leaves a ribbon trail when the beater is lifted. Take from the heat and beat until cool. If using an electric beater, no heat is needed.

Add enough water to the lemon juice to make $\frac{1}{4}$ cup, sprinkle over the gelatin and let stand 5 minutes until spongy. Dissolve the gelatin over a pan of hot water and stir it into the egg mixture. Chill the bowl over a pan of ice water stirring gently until the mixture is on the point of setting, then fold in the lightly whipped cream and the browned breadcrumbs. Pour into the prepared mold, cover and chill at least 2 hours or until set.

To make the sauce: heat the $\frac{1}{4}$ cup sugar with the water until dissolved, then bring to a boil and simmer 2 minutes. Add the plums and cook until very soft. Work the mixture through a sieve or purée it in a blender, then add more sugar to taste. Chill.

A short time before serving, unmold the mousse onto a deep platter, spoon over some of the sauce and serve the rest separately.

Brown bread caramel mousse is served with plum sauce

Peach Soufflé

1 $\frac{1}{2}$ cups peach purée (made with about 4 fresh or canned peaches)
4 eggs, separated
$\frac{1}{4}$ cup sugar
juice of $\frac{1}{2}$ lemon
1 envelope gelatin
$\frac{1}{4}$ teaspoon almond extract
$\frac{3}{4}$ cup heavy cream, whipped until it holds a soft shape

For decoration
$\frac{1}{2}$ cup heavy cream, stiffly whipped
$\frac{1}{4}$ cup chopped pistachios

Soufflé dish (3 cup capacity); pastry bag and medium star tube

Method

Prepare soufflé dish with a paper collar.

Put egg yolks, sugar and peach purée in a bowl and beat until mixed. Set the bowl over a pan of hot but not boiling water and beat until mixture is light and thick and leaves a ribbon trail when the beater is lifted. Take from heat and beat until cool. If using an electric beater, no heat is needed.

Add enough water to the lemon juice to make $\frac{1}{4}$ cup, sprinkle over gelatin and let stand 5 minutes until spongy. Dissolve gelatin over a pan of hot water and stir into the peach mixture with almond extract. Chill bowl over pan of ice water and stir gently until mixture is on the point of setting. Beat egg whites until they hold a stiff peak.

Fold the lightly whipped cream into the peach mixture, then fold in the egg whites and pour mixture into the prepared dish. Chill at least 2 hours or until set.

Shortly before serving, put stiffly whipped cream into pastry bag fitted with the star tube. Carefully peel off the paper collar and decorate the top of the soufflé with rosettes of whipped cream. Press finely chopped pistachios around the side and serve.

Pineapple Mousse en Surprise

3 eggs
2 egg yolks
$\frac{1}{3}$ cup sugar
juice of 1 lemon
1 envelope gelatin
$\frac{1}{2}$ cup unsweetened pineapple juice
1 egg white
$\frac{1}{2}$ cup heavy cream, whipped until it holds a soft shape

For filling
1 medium fresh pineapple or 1 can (8 oz) pineapple rings, drained
4 large macaroons, crumbled
2 tablespoons kirsch or juice from pineapple
$\frac{1}{2}$ cup heavy cream, stiffly whipped

Soufflé dish (1 quart capacity); pastry bag and medium star tube

Method

Prepare soufflé dish with a paper collar and set an oiled tall glass or bottle in the center.

To make the mousse: put the eggs, egg yolks and sugar in a bowl and beat until mixed. Set the bowl over a pan of hot but not boiling water and beat until the mixture is thick and light and leaves a ribbon trail when the beater is lifted. Take from heat and beat until cool. If using an electric beater, no heat is necessary.

Add enough cold water to the lemon juice to make $\frac{1}{4}$ cup, sprinkle over the gelatin and let stand 5 minutes until spongy. Dissolve the gelatin over a pan of hot water and stir into the egg mixture with the pineapple juice. Stiffly whip the egg white.

Chill bowl over a pan of ice water and stir gently until the mixture is on the point of setting. Fold in the lightly whipped cream and egg white and pour at once into the prepared soufflé dish. Cover and chill at least 2 hours or until set.

To make the filling: if using fresh pineapple, cut the base and plume off the pineapple and peel it, removing the core with an apple corer. Slice half the pineapple thinly and cut each slice in half; cut the remaining pineapple in chunks. If using canned pineapple, carefully cut half the slices into 2 rings, then halve each ring. Cut remaining pineapple in chunks.

Mix the pineapple chunks with macaroon crumbs and kirsch or pineapple juice, cover and leave to macerate.

A short time before serving, remove the glass or bottle from the center of the mousse and fill the space with the macaroon mixture. Spread a little whipped cream on top of the mousse and mark a lattice with the point of a knife. Put the remaining cream in a pastry bag fitted with a star tube and pipe rosettes of cream around the top of the mousse. Decorate the rosettes with half slices of pineapple.

Pour pineapple mousse mixture into prepared mold; a few ice cubes inside the jar help to set the mixture quickly

When pineapple mousse is set, carefully lift out the jar

Fill center of mousse with pineapple and macaroon mixture

Soufflé Moka Praliné

- $1\frac{1}{2}$ tablespoons dry instant coffee, dissolved in 6 tablespoons boiling water
- 4 eggs, separated
- $\frac{1}{2}$ cup sugar
- 1 envelope gelatin
- $\frac{1}{4}$ cup water
- 1 cup cream, whipped until it holds a soft shape
- $\frac{1}{2}$ cup heavy cream, stiffly whipped (for decoration)

For praline
- $\frac{1}{2}$ cup almonds
- $\frac{1}{2}$ cup sugar

Soufflé dish ($1\frac{1}{2}$ pint capacity); pastry bag and medium star tube

Method

To prepare praline: put almonds and sugar in a small heavy saucepan and melt sugar over gentle heat. As the sugar starts to caramelize, stir it gently so the almonds cook evenly. When the mixture is dark brown, pour it onto an oiled baking sheet and cool. When cold and brittle grind the praline in a rotary cheese grater or work it in a blender, a little at a time. Prepare dish with a paper collar.

Put egg yolks, sugar and dissolved coffee in a bowl and beat until mixed. Set the bowl over a pan of hot but not boiling water and beat until mixture is thick and leaves a ribbon trail when the beater is lifted. Take from heat and beat until cool. If using an electric beater, no heat is needed.

Sprinkle gelatin over the water and let stand 5 minutes until spongy. Dissolve gelatin over a pan of hot water and stir into the coffee mixture. Chill bowl over pan of ice water and stir gently until mixture is on point of setting. Beat egg whites until they hold a stiff peak. Fold the lightly whipped cream into the coffee mixture with half the praline, then fold in egg whites and pour mixture into prepared dish. Chill at least 2 hours or until set.

To decorate: cut five $\frac{3}{4}$ inch strips of wax paper about 7–8 inches long. Shortly before serving, remove collar from the dish and lay the strips about $\frac{3}{4}$ inch apart, on top of the soufflé. Thickly sprinkle the top with praline, then lift the paper to expose the soufflé underneath. Press remaining praline around the sides of the soufflé. Put the stiffly whipped cream into pastry bag fitted with the star tube and pipe rosettes of cream around the edge of the soufflé.

For moka soufflé: beat egg yolks, sugar and dissolved coffee with an electric beater

Decorate soufflé moka praliné with rosettes of whipped cream and crushed praline

Flan d'Antilles is filled with sliced bananas and covered with orange-flavored cream (recipe is on page 72)

BANANA FLAN COMPLETES A HEARTY DINNER

Try scallops baked with a vegetable mirepoix as an appetizer, or a creamy turnip soup. Cook leg of lamb with a touch of spice and serve with tiny flageolet beans. Choose either a banana flan or almond porcupine cake to complete this tempting menu.

The exciting treatment of a leg of lamb calls for a robust red wine with sufficient zest to match the spices. An ideal candidate would be one of the reds from Yugoslavia that are increasingly available in this country. Among the best is Prokupac (pronounced pro-kew-pats), a warm, rich-flavored wine of great individuality. If this Serbian favorite has not yet reached your area you will be more than happy with the widely available Zinfandel – California's most prolific quality wine whose origins are believed to be Eastern European.

Coquilles St. Jacques Armoricaine
or
Potage Fréneuse
(Cream of Turnip Soup)

Braised Spiced Leg of Lamb
Flageolets Toulousaine *Maître d'Hôtel Potatoes*

Flan d'Antilles
or
Almond Porcupine Cake

Red wine – Prokupac (Yugoslavia)
or Zinfandel (California)

TIMETABLE

Day before
Mix spices for the lamb and rub them into the meat; cover and refrigerate.
Make French flan pastry dough and store in a plastic bag in refrigerator.

Morning
Make turnip soup but do not add liaison; keep in refrigerator.
Braise leg of lamb and leave with gravy in casserole ready for reheating.
Prepare croûtons or cheese puffs to garnish the soup.
Prepare scallops, coat with sauce and leave in their shells or baking dishes ready for browning.
Peel potatoes and leave covered with cold water.
Roll out pastry dough, line flan ring and bake blind.
Rub sugar cubes on the orange rind and crush; squeeze oranges, add juice to sugar cubes and reserve orange syrup for adding to cream. *Or make cake for almond porcupine cake.*

Assemble ingredients for final cooking from 7 p.m. for dinner around 8 p.m.

Order of Work

7:00
Set oven at moderate (350°F).
Slice bananas, fill flan shell, cover with orange-flavored whipped cream and chill. *Or make vanilla pastry cream for cake; let cool.*

7:10
Put lamb in oven to reheat.
Boil potatoes.

7:30
Drain and slice potatoes, arrange in serving dish and keep warm. Prepare butter for potatoes but do not add.
Complete almond porcupine cake.

7:45
Transfer lamb to a hot platter and keep warm. Pour gravy into a gravy boat and keep hot. Cook flageolets.
Reheat soup and add liaison; reheat croûtons, if serving.
Broil the scallops or brown in a hot oven (400°F).
Pour butter over maître d'hôtel potatoes and keep warm.

8:00
Serve appetizer.

You will find that **cooking times** given in the individual recipes for these dishes have sometimes been adapted in the timetable to help you when cooking and serving this menu as a party meal.

Appetizer

Coquilles St. Jacques Armoricaine

1 lb sea scallops
squeeze of lemon juice
4–6 peppercorns
1 bay leaf
2 tablespoons butter
1 carrot, finely diced
2 stalks of celery, finely diced
1 large or 2 small leeks, thinly sliced
2 tablespoons white wine or water, or 1 large tomato, peeled, seeded and chopped
salt and pepper
1–2 tablespoons grated Cheddar or Gruyère cheese

For white sauce
1 tablespoon butter
1 tablespoon flour
1 cup milk

4 scallop shells or individual baking dishes

Method
Put scallops in a saucepan, cover with cold water, add lemon juice, peppercorns and bay leaf and bring to a boil. Reduce heat and poach 5–7 minutes or until the scallops have no transparent center when sliced.

Set the oven at moderate (350°F).

In a flameproof casserole melt the butter, add the carrot, celery and leek and cook over low heat for 3–4 minutes. Add the wine, water or chopped tomato and seasoning, cover and bake the mirepoix in the heated oven for 5–6 minutes.

Put a spoonful of the mirepoix into each scallop shell or dish. Drain the scallops, slice them and lay these on top of the mirepoix.

Make the white sauce, adding to it any juice from the mirepoix and season it. Spoon sauce over scallops, sprinkle with grated cheese and brown under the broiler or in a very hot oven (450°F). Serve at once.

Alternative appetizer

Potage Fréneuse (Cream of Turnip Soup)

3–4 (1 lb) medium white turnips, sliced
1 medium onion, sliced
2 medium potatoes, sliced
3 tablespoons butter
1 tablespoon flour
6–7 cups chicken or vegetable stock
salt and pepper
fried croûtons or small cheese puffs (to serve)

For liaison
2 egg yolks, or 1 teaspoon arrowroot
$\frac{1}{2}$ cup light cream

If using yellow turnips, use only $\frac{3}{4}$ lb; blanch after slicing to remove the strong flavor.

Method
In a kettle melt the butter, add the turnips, onion and potatoes and press a piece of buttered foil on top. Add the lid and 'sweat' the vegetables – cook them very gently in their own juices over low heat for 8–10 minutes; do not let them brown.

Take pan from heat, stir in flour and pour in the stock.

Coquilles St. Jacques Armoricaine are sprinkled with grated cheese before being browned and served very hot in shells

Bring to a boil, stirring, cover and simmer 35–40 minutes or until the vegetables are very soft. Work them through a sieve or food mill or purée them in a blender. Return to the pan and reheat.

To prepare liaison: mix egg yolks or arrowroot with cream. Stir a little of the hot soup into the mixture and add this to remaining soup.

Heat, stirring, until soup thickens slightly; if using an egg yolk liaison, do not let soup boil or it will curdle. Season to taste; serve with croûtons or small cheese puffs.

Cheese Puffs

Make a small quantity of choux pastry in the following proportions (be sure to measure accurately): $\frac{1}{2}$ cup flour, pinch of salt, $\frac{1}{2}$ cup water, $\frac{1}{4}$ cup butter and 2 eggs. Stir in $\frac{1}{4}$ cup grated Parmesan cheese.

Spoon dough into a pastry bag fitted with a $\frac{1}{4}$ inch plain tube and pipe tiny mounds on a dampened baking sheet. Bake in a hot oven (400°F) for 12–15 minutes or until the puffs are brown and crisp. Cool before serving.

Serve braised spiced leg of lamb with flageolets Toulousaine – small green kidney beans – and maître d'hôtel potatoes

Entrée

Braised Spiced Leg of Lamb

1 small ($3\frac{1}{2}$–4 lb) leg of lamb
2 teaspoons ground coriander
1 teaspoon ground cumin
$\frac{1}{2}$ teaspoon ground ginger
1 teaspoon paprika
1 teaspoon salt
$\frac{1}{2}$ teaspoon pepper
2 tablespoons oil
2 tablespoons butter
1 large carrot, sliced
1 large onion, sliced
2 stalks of celery, sliced
1–$1\frac{1}{2}$ cups beef stock
bouquet garni
1 teaspoon tomato paste
kneaded butter (made with 1 tablespoon butter, $1\frac{1}{2}$ teaspoons flour)

Method

Mix the spices with salt and pepper and rub them into the leg of lamb. Let the meat stand at least 1–2 hours, or refrigerate it overnight.

To braise lamb, in a large flameproof casserole heat the oil and butter, put in the lamb and brown it slowly on all sides.

Watchpoint: do not brown lamb too much or the spices will scorch and lose their flavor.

Remove the lamb and add all the vegetables, cover and cook over a low heat for 5–7 minutes. Replace lamb in the casserole, add stock, bouquet garni and tomato paste. Cover tightly and braise in a moderate oven (350°F) for $1\frac{1}{2}$–2 hours or until meat is very tender.

Remove the lamb from the pot and strain cooking liquid into a pan. Whisk in kneaded butter and bring to a boil, stirring constantly until the gravy thickens. Replace lamb in pot, spoon over some gravy, cover and keep warm. Serve with flageolets Toulousaine and maître d'hôtel potatoes.

To prepare ahead: leave lamb in the gravy, then reheat in a moderate oven (350°F) for 30–40 minutes.

Spoon the mixed spices over leg of lamb, rub in well and let meat stand; sliced carrot, onion and celery are ready for braising

Accompaniment to entrée

Flageolets Toulousaine

1 can (15 oz) flageolets, drained
1 tablespoon oil or butter
2 cloves of garlic, crushed
3 tomatoes, peeled, seeded and chopped
salt and pepper

Flageolets are delicious, small green kidney beans, grown and used extensively in France. Here they are generally available dried and in cans.

Method

In a saucepan or flameproof casserole heat the oil or butter, add the garlic and tomatoes and cook until they are pulpy. Add the drained flageolets and season. Cover and simmer over a low heat for 7–10 minutes or until all the ingredients are hot and thoroughly blended.

Add drained beans to garlic-flavored tomato pulp for the flageolets Toulousaine to accompany the braised spiced leg of lamb

Dessert

Flan d'Antilles

For French flan pastry
scant 1½ cups flour
6 tablespoons butter
6 tablespoons sugar
3 egg yolks
1 teaspoon vanilla

For filling
10 sugar cubes
2 large oranges
4 ripe bananas
1 cup heavy cream, whipped until it holds a soft shape

8 inch flan ring

Method

To make French flan pastry: sift the flour onto a board or marble slab and make a large well in the center. Add the butter, sugar, egg yolks and vanilla and work together with the fingertips until smooth. Gradually draw in flour, working with the whole hand to form a smooth dough. Chill dough for 1 hour, roll out and line the flan ring; bake blind in a moderately hot oven (375°F) for 15–20 minutes or until pastry is lightly browned.

Rub the sugar cubes over the skin of the oranges until they are saturated with the oil; squeeze the oranges and strain the juice. Crush sugar cubes and add orange juice to dissolve the sugar. Thinly slice the bananas and moisten them with half of the orange syrup. Spread them in the baked flan shell. Beat the rest of the orange mixture into the cream, spread over bananas and serve.

Work the sugar, butter, egg yolks and vanilla together, then draw in the flour to make a firm dough

Spoon the thinly-sliced bananas in orange syrup into flan shell; cover with orange-flavored whipped cream

Alternative dessert

Almond Porcupine Cake

For cake
⅔ cup sugar
3 eggs, separated
grated rind and juice of 1 lemon
¾ cup cake flour
¾ cup whole blanched almonds, ground

For vanilla pastry cream
1 egg, separated
1 egg yolk
¼ cup sugar
1½ tablespoons cornstarch
1½ cups milk
½ teaspoon vanilla
juice of ½ orange

To finish
½ cup slivered almonds
¼ cup Cointreau liqueur

Ring mold (1 quart capacity)

Method

Grease the ring mold, sprinkle it with sugar, then with flour and discard the excess. Set the oven at moderate (350°F).

To make the cake: beat ½ cup of the sugar with the egg yolks until the mixture is thick and light. Add the grated lemon rind and juice and continue beating until the mixture thickens again slightly. Sift the flour and stir in the ground almonds. Stiffly whip the egg whites, add the remaining sugar and continue beating until this meringue is glossy. Fold the egg whites into the lemon mixture alternately with the almonds and flour. Spoon the batter into the prepared pan and bake in the heated oven for 35–40 minutes or until the cake springs back when lightly pressed with a fingertip. Transfer to a wire rack to cool.

Make the vanilla pastry cream (see page 88), cover and let it cool.

A short time before serving, set the cake in a shallow dish and stud it all over with slivered almonds to represent spines. Spoon over the liqueur and pile the pastry cream in the center.

A hearty dinner

Almond porcupine cake is studded with slivered almonds to represent spines, and vanilla pastry cream is piled in the center

Sole Catalan – fillets are arranged, overlapping, on rice salad, then coated with mayonnaise and decorated with crosses of pimiento. Garnish with watercress

CLASSIC FISH DISHES (1)

Over the years innumerable recipes have been developed to take advantage of the versatility of fish. Fish can be cooked whole or boned, it can be stuffed or coated with a sauce, or fish fillets may be called for in a recipe. Frequently one kind of fish can be substituted for another providing it is similar in size and flavor. Haddock, for instance, can be used instead of cod; flounder or any white fish fillets are a substitute for sole. However, a few fish – e.g. trout and salmon – have no close equivalents so it is better not to substitute.

There are two basic rules for fish dishes – fish must be very fresh if its flavor is to be fully appreciated, and it must never be overcooked – it cooks in a surprisingly short time.

To Fold Fish Fillets

Fillets may be folded in two ways and neat folding makes a great difference to the appearance of the finished dish.

When using long fillets, fold the fillet in three, skinned side inside, tucking the tip of the tail under the head end; make sure that all fillets are folded to the same length even if originally they were different lengths.

If the fillets are short and wide, fold them in half across, skinned side inside, and tail on top, bringing the tail end to meet the head.

Fold long fish fillets in three, skinned side inside, tucking tip of the tail under head end

Fold short fillets in half across, skinned side inside, bringing the tail end to meet the head

To Flatten Fish Fillets

Many classic fish recipes call for stuffing fillets. To prevent the fish from shrinking during cooking, the fillets should be flattened lightly.

Place fillets between 2 sheets of wax paper and, with a cutlet bat or the base of a skillet or heavy saucepan, hit the fillet hard so it flattens and spreads out about $\frac{1}{4}$ inch all around. Spread the skinned side of the fillet with stuffing and fold in two or three.

Note: recipes in this feature serve 4 people as an entrée or 6 people as an appetizer, with the exception of recipes using whole fish like trout, when 1 fish serves 1 person.

Sole Caprice

$1\frac{1}{2}$ lb fillets of sole
$\frac{1}{2}$ cup melted butter
$1\frac{1}{2}$–2 cups fresh white breadcrumbs
salt and pepper
2 bananas
squeeze of lemon juice
$1\frac{1}{2}$ cups well-seasoned tomato sauce

Method

Wash and dry the fish fillets on paper towels. Dip fillets in melted butter, then coat them thickly with breadcrumbs, pressing them on with a metal spatula. Place the fillets on the rack of a broiler pan, baste with more melted butter, sprinkle with seasoning and broil 4–5 inches from the heat for 7–8 minutes, turning them once and basting once or twice with butter in the pan.

Peel and slice the bananas diagonally into large pieces. Sauté them in the remaining butter, sprinkled with lemon juice, for 4–5 minutes or until golden brown.

Arrange the fish fillets on a hot platter, set a slice of banana on top of each one, and serve the hot tomato sauce separately.

Watchpoint: the tomato sauce should be made with very little flour so it is clear red and not too thick.

Sole Catalan

$1\frac{1}{2}$ lb fillets of sole
court bouillon (made with $\frac{3}{4}$ cup water, slice of onion, 6 peppercorns, 1 bay leaf and $\frac{1}{4}$ teaspoon salt)
mayonnaise (made with 2 egg yolks, 1 cup olive oil, about 2 tablespoons vinegar or lemon juice, salt and pepper, pinch of dry mustard)
$\frac{1}{2}$ small clove of garlic, crushed
1 teaspoon tomato paste
$\frac{1}{2}$ teaspoon paprika

For rice salad
1 cup rice
1 cucumber, peeled, seeded and diced
$\frac{3}{4}$ cup cooked green peas or cooked green beans, cut in diamond-shaped pieces
$\frac{3}{4}$ cup cooked diced carrots
$\frac{1}{3}$ cup vinaigrette dressing

For garnish
2 slices of canned pimiento, cut in strips, with a little liquid from the can
bunch of watercress

Method

Fold the sole fillets in half and lay them in a buttered baking dish. Add the court bouillon, cover with buttered foil and poach in a moderately low oven (325°F) for 12–15 minutes or until the fish flakes easily when tested with a fork. Take from the oven and let cool in the liquid.

To make rice salad: sprinkle the cucumber with salt and let stand 30 minutes to draw out the juices (dégorger); rinse with cold water and drain on paper towels. Cook the rice in plenty of boiling salted water for 12 minutes or until just tender, drain, rinse with hot water, drain again and spread out in an airy place for 15 minutes to dry. Mix the rice with the cucumber, cooked vegetables and vinaigrette dressing and season to taste.

Make the mayonnaise and add the garlic, tomato paste, paprika, and reserved pimiento juice to taste. Thin mayonnaise, if necessary, with boiling water until it coats the back of a spoon.

Arrange the rice salad down the center of a serving dish. Drain the fish fillets thoroughly on paper towels and arrange them, overlapping, on top of the salad. Coat the fish with mayonnaise and decorate the top of each fillet with a cross of pimiento. Garnish the dish with watercress and serve remaining mayonnaise separately.

Sole Nantua

1½ lb fillets of sole
mousseline stuffing (see right), with ½ lb uncooked peeled shrimps added (shells reserved for mayonnaise collée)
squeeze of lemon juice
2–3 tablespoons fish stock or water

For mayonnaise collée
shrimp shells
1 cup olive oil
½ teaspoon paprika
1–1½ tablespoons lemon juice
2 egg yolks
½ envelope gelatin
¼ cup cool but still liquid fish aspic (see page 31)

For garnish
4 large cooked peeled shrimps
1½ cups cool but still liquid fish aspic
bunch of watercress

Method

Make the mousseline stuffing with the shrimps.

Wash and dry the fillets of sole, flatten them slightly and spread mousseline stuffing on the skinned sides. Fold the fish fillets, lay them in a large baking dish, squeeze over the lemon juice and add fish stock or water. Cover with buttered paper and bake in a moderate oven (350°F) for 15 minutes or until fish flakes easily. Drain fillets on paper towels and let cool.

To make mayonnaise collée: wash and dry shrimp shells and pound them with the olive oil and paprika or work them for a few seconds in a blender; let stand 10–15 minutes, then squeeze through cheesecloth and use this oil with the lemon juice and egg yolks to make mayonnaise in the usual way. Season to taste. Sprinkle the gelatin over the ¼ cup of cool but still liquid fish aspic, let stand 5 minutes until soft, then dissolve over a pan of hot water. Let cool to tepid and stir into the mayonnaise.

Place fish fillets on a wire rack and chill thoroughly. Stir the mayonnaise collée over a pan of ice water until it is on the point of setting, then spoon it over the fish fillets to coat them. Chill and add a second coating of mayonnaise, if necessary.

To garnish: set a cooked, peeled shrimp on top of each fish fillet and chill. Stir the 1½ cups cool but still liquid fish aspic over a bowl of ice water until on the point of setting, then spoon enough over the fish fillets to coat them. Chill and add a second coat, if necessary. Chill until the aspic is firmly set. Pour the remaining aspic into a tray, chill until set, then chop it.

Spread the chopped aspic on a silver or stainless steel platter, arrange the fish fillets on top and garnish the platter with watercress.

Mousseline Stuffing

½ lb perch, whitefish or flounder fillets
2 egg whites
¾ cup heavy cream
salt and pepper

Makes enough to fill 1½ lb of fish fillets.

Method

Wash and dry fish and remove any bones. Pass the fish twice through the fine blade of a grinder, then pound (with the shrimps if preparing sole Nantua) until smooth in a mortar and pestle and gradually work in the egg whites.

Or, instead of pounding, work the fish and shrimps, if using, with the egg whites for a few seconds in a blender until very smooth.

Gradually beat in the cream, then add seasoning.

Sole en Eventail

1½ lb fillets of sole
mousseline stuffing
juice of ½ lemon

For mayonnaise collée
1 cup mayonnaise
½ envelope gelatin
¼ cup cool but still liquid fish aspic (see page 31)

For garnish
3–4 small mushrooms, finely sliced
squeeze of lemon juice
3–4 cups cool but still liquid fish aspic

Eventail means 'fan' in French and refers to the arrangement of food in a fan shape.

Method

Make mousseline stuffing.

Wash and dry the sole fillets, flatten them slightly and spread the stuffing on the skinned sides. Fold over the tail section, tucking the flat end under, and smooth the sides; make sure that each fillet is pointed at the end. Arrange the fillets in a lightly buttered baking dish, sprinkle with lemon juice, cover with buttered foil and bake in a moderate oven (350°F) for 15 minutes or until the fish flakes easily. Drain the fillets on paper towels and cool.

To make mayonnaise collée: sprinkle the gelatin over the ¼ cup aspic, let stand 5 minutes until soft and dissolve over a pan of hot water. Stir into the mayonnaise.

Set the fish fillets on a wire rack and chill thoroughly. Stir the mayonnaise collée over a bowl of ice water until it is on the point of setting and spoon it quickly over the fillets to coat them. Chill and add a second coating, if necessary. Chill until firmly set.

To prepare garnish: put the sliced mushrooms in a buttered pan, sprinkle with lemon juice and seasoning, cover tightly with foil and the lid and cook gently until mushrooms are soft.

Dip the mushroom slices in aspic, arrange 2 on top of each fish fillet and chill. Stir 2 cups remaining fish aspic over a bowl of ice water until on the point of setting, then spoon over the fish fillets to coat them. Chill and add a second coat, if necessary. Chill until the aspic is firmly set. Pour the remaining aspic into a tray, chill until set. Cut half the aspic layer into triangles or squares and chop the rest.

Spread the chopped aspic along one side of an oval silver or stainless steel platter and place the fish fillets on top in a fan shape. Arrange the diamonds or triangles of aspic in center of dish and garnish with a bunch of watercress.

Sole en éventail is coated with mayonnaise collée and arranged on chopped aspic in a fan shape (recipe is on page 77)

Salmon Steaks aux Gourmets

4 salmon steaks, cut 1 inch thick
1 cup white wine
squeeze of lemon juice
slice of onion
6 peppercorns
few stalks of parsley

For hollandaise sauce
$\frac{1}{4}$ cup white wine vinegar (seasoned with slice of onion, 6 peppercorns, blade of mace and small bay leaf)
3 egg yolks
$\frac{3}{4}$ cup unsalted butter
salt and pepper
1–2 tablespoons light cream

For garnish
1 cup ($\frac{1}{4}$ lb) mushrooms, sliced
1 tablespoon butter
squeeze of lemon juice
salt and pepper
1 teaspoon tomato paste
grated rind of $\frac{1}{2}$ orange
4 medium tomatoes, peeled, seeded and cut in strips

Method

Wash and dry salmon steaks. Set them in a baking dish, pour over the wine and lemon juice, add onion, peppercorns and parsley, and cover with buttered foil. Poach in a moderate oven (350°F) for 15–20 minutes or until the fish flakes easily.

To make hollandaise sauce: reduce the vinegar with its seasonings to a scant tablespoon. With a wooden spoon beat the egg yolks in a bowl with $\frac{1}{2}$ tablespoon butter and a pinch of salt until light and slightly thick. Strain on the vinegar, set bowl over a pan of boiling water, turn off heat and add remaining butter in small pieces, stirring. Add cream, taste for seasoning and keep warm in water bath.

To prepare garnish: sauté mushrooms in butter with lemon juice until tender.

Drain salmon steaks on paper towels; strain the cooking liquid and reduce it to 1 tablespoon. Remove the skin from the steaks and lift out the bones, keeping the steaks as intact as possible; keep them warm on a platter.

Stir the reduced cooking liquid with the tomato paste and orange rind into the hollandaise sauce, add the mushrooms and tomatoes, taste for seasoning, and spoon over salmon steaks. If you like, broil them quickly to glaze.

Red Snapper Basquaise

4 medium red snapper fillets or 4 red snapper steaks, cut 1 inch thick
$\frac{3}{4}$ cup water
$\frac{1}{2}$ cup white wine
squeeze of lemon juice
salt and pepper
$1\frac{1}{2}$ cups mayonnaise
1 teaspoon tomato paste
1 clove of garlic, crushed

For garnish
2 red bell peppers
2 cups (8 oz) mushrooms, thickly sliced
2 tablespoons oil
$\frac{1}{3}$ cup vinaigrette dressing
$\frac{1}{2}$ lb cooked peeled, medium shrimps

Method

Wash and dry the fish, place it in a buttered baking dish and add the water, wine, lemon juice and seasoning. Cover with buttered foil and poach in a moderate oven (350°F) for 15–20 minutes or until fish flakes easily. Let cool in liquid.

To make garnish: peel the peppers by first broiling them or piercing them with a long fork and holding over a gas flame, turning them until the skin is charred and easy to peel. Then rinse peppers with cold water to stop them from cooking, peel, remove the cores and seeds and cut flesh in strips. In a skillet heat the oil, add the mushrooms and peppers and sauté 1 minute. Mix them in a bowl with the vinaigrette dressing.

Drain fish on paper towels and, if using steaks, remove skin and bones, keeping steaks as intact as possible. Arrange fish on a platter.

Strain the cooking liquid and add enough to the mayonnaise to thin it so it coats the back of a spoon. Add the tomato paste and garlic and season to taste. Add half the mayonnaise to the shrimps (chop them coarsely if they are large) and spoon over the fish to coat it. Garnish the dish with mushrooms and peppers and serve remaining mayonnaise separately.

The Basque country lies at the northern end of the Pyrenees, partly in Spain, partly in France, and the cooking of the region is influenced by both countries. In red snapper Basquaise, for example, garlic and peppers are typical Spanish ingredients but the elaborate treatment of the fish is French.

Note: recipes in this lesson serve 4 people as an entrée or 6 people as an appetizer, with the exception of recipes using whole fish like trout, when 1 fish serves 1 person.

Stuffed Trout

4 trout ($\frac{3}{4}$ lb–1 lb each)
$\frac{1}{4}$ cup melted butter

For mousseline stuffing
1 lb perch, whitefish or flounder fillets
3 egg whites
1 cup heavy cream
salt and pepper

To finish
1–2 shallots, finely chopped
3 tablespoons butter
$\frac{1}{2}$ cup white wine
1 teaspoon brandy
1 tablespoon chopped parsley

Method

Make the mousseline stuffing (see page 77).

Wash and dry trout, bone them (see page 80) and spread the mousseline stuffing inside; reshape and lift them carefully into a shallow buttered baking dish. Pour over melted butter, sprinkle with a little salt and pepper and bake in a moderate oven (350°F) for 20–25 minutes or until they flake easily. Then broil them 2–3 minutes until the skin is crisp and brown and keep warm.

To finish: cook shallots in butter until they are just beginning to brown. Add wine and salt and pepper and boil rapidly for 1 minute; stir in brandy and parsley, pour over trout and serve at once.

To Bone Trout

Trout can be boned before or after cooking.

To Bone a Raw Trout

Snip off the fins with scissors and 'vandyke' the tail by cutting it into a 'V'. Cut off the head with a sharp knife and slit down the back, keeping the knife on top of and touching the backbone; open the fish until it lies flat on the board. Insert the knife under the backbone at the head end and cut the bone away from the flesh, working towards the tail with short strokes of the knife; discard backbone.

To Bone a Cooked Trout

Carefully remove and discard the skin (this is easiest when the trout is warm), then insert a knife along the back and gently detach the flesh from the bone. Snip the backbone at the head – this is usually left on cooked trout – and tail with scissors and pull out the bone sideways, starting at the tail.

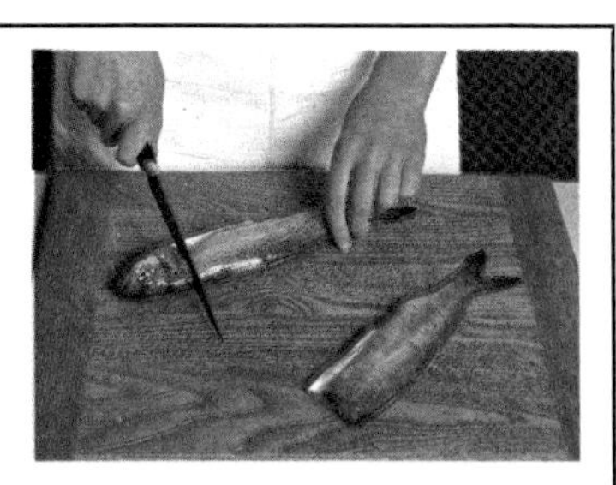

To bone a raw trout: cut off the head, then slit down the back; using a sharp knife and keeping the blade near to the bone, ease flesh off backbone and open out fish

To bone a cooked trout: with scissors, cut away the skin at the head and tail; gently pull out the backbone, sideways, starting at the tail end; leave head on

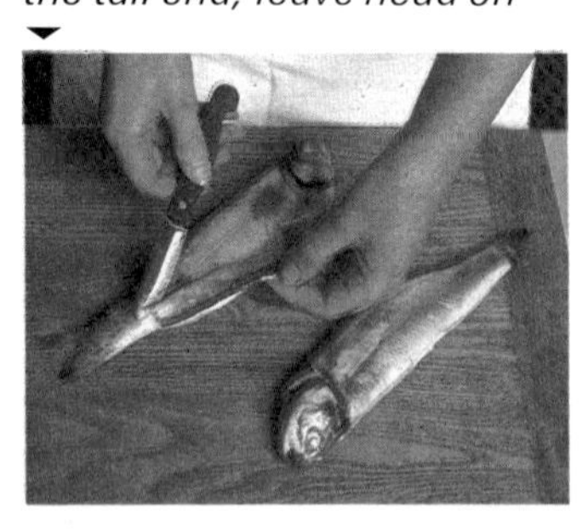

Trout Belin

4 trout ($\frac{3}{4}$–1 lb each)
$\frac{1}{4}$ cup seasoned flour (made with $\frac{1}{4}$ teaspoon salt, pinch of pepper)
6 tablespoons butter
juice of 1 lemon
juice of 1 orange
1 tablespoon chopped parsley

For stuffing
$\frac{3}{4}$ lb fresh spinach or 1 package frozen spinach
1 tablespoon chopped parsley
1 teaspoon mixed herbs (chervil, tarragon, chives)
4 shallots, finely chopped
3 tablespoons butter
2 cups ($\frac{1}{2}$ lb) mushrooms, finely chopped
salt and pepper

For garnish
1 large orange, sliced
1 tablespoon butter
2 teaspoons sugar
bunch of watercress

Method

To make the stuffing: if using fresh spinach, wash, drain, remove the stems and blanch in boiling water for 1 minute, then drain. Defrost and drain frozen spinach. Chop spinach and mix with parsley and herbs. In a skillet sauté the shallot in butter until soft, add mushrooms and spinach, season, cover the pan and cook gently 5–6 minutes. Let the stuffing cool.

Bone the raw trout, fill them with the stuffing and reshape. Coat fish carefully in seasoned flour. In a skillet melt 3 tablespoons butter and sauté trout over medium heat for 4–5 minutes on each side or until golden brown and fish flakes easily. Season lightly and keep warm on a serving platter.

To prepare garnish: wipe out the pan, melt the 1 tablespoon butter and add the orange slices, sprinkle them with half the sugar, turn over and sauté briskly until browned. Sprinkle with the remaining sugar, turn over, brown on the other side and place 1–2 slices on each trout or overlap the slices around edge of serving dish.

Wipe out the pan, add remaining butter and cook to a nut-brown (noisette). At once add lemon and orange juice with the parsley and pour sauce over fish while it is still foaming. Garnish the dish with watercress and serve.

Note: recipes in this feature serve 4 people as an entrée or 6 people as an appetizer, with the exception of recipes using whole fish like trout, when 1 fish serves 1 person.

Classic fish dishes (1)

Trout Belin, with spinach and herb stuffing, are garnished with orange slices sautéed in butter and watercress

Gâteau au chocolat is decorated with scrolls of chocolate caraque and sprinkled with confectioners' sugar (recipe is on page 89)

FRENCH GATEAUX AND PASTRIES

Although the art of making gâteaux and pastries took hundreds of years to develop in France it is not as complicated as the splendor of the finished products might suggest. Classic pastries and gâteaux are built from several simple foundation recipes such as Génoise (Genoese) sponge cake and French flan pastry, then filled and decorated with rich mixtures like pastry cream, fondant icing and butter cream frosting. Combinations are traditional and gâteau St. Honoré, for instance – made with French flan pastry, pastry cream and choux pastry cream puffs – can be found in pastry shops all over France.

Decoration forms an important part of all these classic recipes and it is well worth taking the extra trouble to achieve a perfect finish. Butter cream rosettes must all be the same size, icing should be absolutely smooth and almonds for coating must be evenly browned. Be sure to flavor fillings highly with vanilla, coffee or whatever is suggested, otherwise the finished cakes can taste unpleasantly sweet and rich.

The basic recipes for making gâteaux and pastries with fillings and decorations are given first for easy reference, followed by a choice of gâteaux and small pastries.

French Flan Pastry

French flan pastry is made with flour, butter, sugar and egg yolks with no additional liquid. The method of mixing is quite different from regular pie pastry; as a result the dough is firm, without any elasticity, and keeps its shape during baking. The finished pastry is crunchy and melting, like a cookie.

Chill the dough for at least an hour before rolling to make it firm. It can be made a day or two before and kept in the refrigerator. The baking temperature is lower than for pie pastry because of the high sugar content. The pastry is cooked when it is a delicate pale golden; if overbaked it becomes hard and tasteless.

Basic French Flan Pastry

For 1 cup quantity
scant 1 cup flour
$\frac{1}{4}$ cup butter
$\frac{1}{4}$ cup sugar
2 egg yolks
$\frac{1}{2}$ teaspoon vanilla

Makes enough to line a 7–8 inch flan ring, or 9–12 individual tartlet pans (depending on size).

For $\frac{1}{2}$ cup quantity
$\frac{1}{2}$ cup flour
2 tablespoons butter
2 tablespoons sugar
1 egg yolk
$\frac{1}{4}$ teaspoon vanilla

Makes enough for an 8 inch pastry circle or to line 5–6 tartlet pans.

Method

Sift the flour onto a board or marble slab and make a large well in the center. Add the butter, sugar, egg yolks and vanilla, and work together with the fingertips until smooth. Gradually draw in the flour, working with the whole hand to form a dough, then knead lightly until smooth. Chill 1–2 hours before using.

For French flan pastry, put the sugar, egg yolks, butter and vanilla in the well in flour

Vanilla sugar (made by leaving a vanilla bean in a jar of sugar for several days or longer) can be used instead of plain sugar and vanilla extract.

Note: do not reduce quantities to make smaller gâteaux because it is impossible to measure smaller quantities accurately.

Frangipane

1 cup whole blanched almonds, ground
$\frac{1}{2}$ cup butter
$\frac{1}{2}$ cup sugar
2 eggs, beaten to mix
$\frac{1}{4}$ cup flour
orange flower water, lemon juice, kirsch or vanilla (to flavor)

Frangipane can be used in pastries and gâteaux, or it may be baked on its own as a cake. Orange flower water is obtainable at specialty stores and some pharmacies.

Method

Cream the butter, gradually beat in sugar and continue beating until mixture is light and soft. Gradually add the eggs, beating well after each addition. Add the flavoring as required, then stir in ground almonds and flour. Use as specified in the recipe.

To bake as a cake: set oven at moderate (350°F) and grease a 6–7 inch moule à manqué or 6 inch springform pan, then sprinkle with sugar and flour and discard the excess. Pour in the batter and bake in heated oven for 40–45 minutes or until a skewer inserted in the center comes out clean. Turn out on a wire rack to cool.

Frangipane is thought to have been invented by an Italian perfumer named Frangipani who had a very sweet tooth. He lived in Paris during the reign of Louis XIII.

Génoise

Génoise – Genoese sponge cake – batter has a base of beaten eggs and sugar like regular sponge cake, but softened butter is added to make the finished cake richer and give it a closer texture.

Rich Génoise sponge cakes keep well, but they can be tricky to make because the weight of extra butter makes the batter fall unless the mixture is folded together very lightly.

For more general advice read the feature on sponge cakes in Volume 6.

Basic Génoise

For 4 egg quantity
4 eggs
6 tablespoons butter
$\frac{2}{3}$ cup sugar
$\frac{2}{3}$ cup cake flour
pinch of salt
$\frac{1}{2}$ teaspoon vanilla

9–10 inch moule à manqué or 8–9 inch springform pan

For 3 egg quantity
3 eggs
$\frac{1}{4}$ cup butter
$\frac{1}{2}$ cup sugar
$\frac{1}{2}$ cup cake flour
pinch of salt
$\frac{1}{2}$ teaspoon vanilla

8–9 inch moule à manqué or 7–8 inch springform pan

Method

Set oven at moderate (350°F). Grease the mold or pan, line the bottom with a circle of wax paper, grease it again, sprinkle with sugar, then with flour, and discard the excess.

Sift flour and salt 2–3 times. Warm butter in a bowl or pan over hot water until it is very soft and pourable.

Watchpoint: take great care that the butter does not become hot or oily.

Break eggs into a large bowl (preferably copper) and gradually beat in sugar with a balloon whisk, electric beater or rotary beater. Set bowl over a pan of boiling water but not touching the water; take pan from the heat. Beat sugar and eggs for 10–12 minutes or until the mixture is light and thick enough to leave a ribbon trail on itself when the beater is lifted. Take bowl off the pan, add vanilla and continue whisking 5 minutes or until the mixture is cold. If using an electric beater, no heat is necessary.

Sift one-third of the flour over the batter and fold it in with a metal spoon. Next fold in half the remaining flour, then the butter, quickly followed by the remaining flour.

Transfer batter to the prepared pan and bake in heated oven for 25–30 minutes for the smaller cake (3 egg quantity) or 40–45 minutes for the larger one (4 egg quantity), or until cake shrinks slightly from sides of pan and top springs back when lightly pressed with a fingertip. Turn out onto a wire rack to cool.

For Génoise sponge cake, fold in two-thirds of the flour, add the softened butter followed by remaining flour

Lightly fold the cake mixture together with a metal spoon and pour it into prepared pan

To Beat Egg Whites

If possible, use a copper bowl and balloon whisk – their rounded shapes help beat in plenty of air; the copper surface gives egg whites a close, smooth texture.

A copper bowl must be cleaned before use. Put in 2 tablespoons salt with 2 tablespoons vinegar or lemon juice; rub with a cloth until the bowl shines; wash with warm water and dry. Any dampness, grease or specks of yolk on whisk or bowl, will prevent whites from becoming really stiff.

Alternatively, use a stainless steel bowl. Beat whites to a froth only with rotary or electric beater. Finish with balloon whisk.

Quantity Terms

Terms like 1 cup quantity pastry or 1 cup quantity butter cream frosting refer to the amount obtained by using 1 cup of the principal ingredient at the top of the ingredient list, not 1 cup of prepared pastry dough or butter cream frosting.

Choux Pastry

Choux pastry has a high egg content and puffs to 2–3 times its original size during baking. Detailed instructions on making choux pastry were given in Volume 6 but the basic recipe is repeated here for convenience.

Basic Choux Pastry

For 3–4 egg quantity
$\frac{2}{3}$ cup flour
$\frac{1}{4}$ teaspoon salt
$\frac{2}{3}$ cup water
$\frac{1}{3}$ cup butter
3–4 eggs

Method

Sift flour and salt onto a piece of wax paper. Put water and butter in a fairly large saucepan, bring to a boil and when bubbling, draw pan from heat and immediately pour in all the flour. Beat vigorously for a few seconds until mixture is smooth and pulls away from sides of pan to form a ball.

Cool mixture about 5 minutes, then beat in eggs one at a time. If eggs are large, break the last one into a bowl and beat with a fork to mix. Add this slowly to the choux pastry dough to ensure that it remains firm and keeps its shape but will just drop easily from a spoon – all of this last egg may not be needed, depending on the consistency of the dough.

Beat the dough for 1–2 minutes until it is glossy and very smooth. Use as specified in the recipe.

A selection of pans includes from left: moule à manqué and brioche pans, a six-madeleine tray and individual boat molds and tartlet pans in two sizes

To Line Boat Molds or Tartlet Pans

French flan pastry is particularly suitable for lining molds as it is easy to handle when chilled and does not shrink during baking.

Divide pastry dough in half and roll it very thinly. Set 4–5 molds or pans on the work surface. Roll the dough around the rolling pin, lift it up and lay it across the top of the molds. Cut off a small piece of dough and roll it into a ball the size of a marble. Dip the ball lightly in flour and use it to pat and press the dough into the molds, easing it down gently. When the molds are well lined, roll the rolling pin across the top – first one way, then the other – to cut off the dough. With finger and thumb, press up the edge of the dough so it comes up a little above the edge of the mold and the baked pastry shell is deepened. Before baking, prick base of dough to release any trapped air.

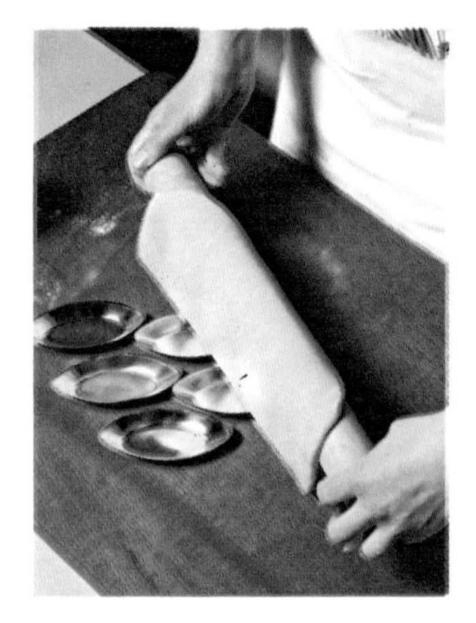

To line boat molds; lay a layer of dough across the molds

Press dough into molds with a lightly floured ball of dough

Roll rolling pin one way, then the other, to cut dough

Molds

Some pastries and gâteaux are made in special molds or pans. For French flan pastry, tartlet molds should be fairly deep and measure 2–2½ inches in diameter; boat molds should be 2½–3 inches long, preferably with a wide base.

Moule à manqué cake pans are deep with sloping sides and some have a pattern on the bottom. They are used for Génoise, regular sponge cakes and other cakes, particularly when the cake is to be iced – the cake is turned upside down so the icing runs down the sloping edges.

Madeleine pans have a characteristic shell shape. The Madeleine mixture is a light sponge batter often flavored with orange flower water or grated lemon rind.

All these pans – sold in most kitchen equipment shops – can be used for other mixtures such as gelatins and molded desserts.

Quantity Terms

Terms like 1 cup quantity pastry or 1 cup quantity butter cream frosting refer to the amount obtained by using 1 cup of the principal ingredient at the top of the ingredient list, not 1 cup of prepared pastry dough or butter cream frosting.

To Line Flan Rings

Set flan ring on a baking sheet (preferably without edges – so flan can be easily removed). Roll out chilled pastry dough, $\frac{1}{4}$ inch thick, into a circle about $1\frac{1}{2}$ inches larger than the flan ring. Roll dough around rolling pin and lay it over flan ring, overlapping the edge. Ease down quickly so it does not break.

Press dough into ring with a dough ball, as for boat molds, letting excess rest over edge of ring. Pass rolling pin over the top to cut off excess. Pinch around edge with forefinger and thumb, then with fingers push dough evenly up the sides, working from bottom of ring, to increase height of edge. Prick base of dough to release trapped air before baking.

Fillings and Decorations

Butter Cream Frosting

Two kinds of butter cream frosting are used in pastries and gâteaux. The first is made with a fluffy egg yolk and sugar mixture, beaten into softened butter. For the second, softened butter is added to meringue to make a frosting that is slightly less rich and paler so it is good for pastel colors. Always use unsalted butter for butter cream frosting since even a touch of salt will give an unpleasant taste.

Butter Cream Frosting 1

For $\frac{3}{4}$ cup quantity
$\frac{3}{4}$ cup unsalted butter
2 egg yolks
$\frac{1}{4}$ cup sugar
$\frac{1}{4}$ cup water

To flavor (optional)
1 teaspoon vanilla
grated rind of $\frac{1}{2}$ orange or 1 lemon
2 teaspoons dry instant coffee dissolved in a little water
2–3 squares (2–3 oz) semisweet chocolate, melted over hot water and left until cool but still liquid

Method

In a bowl beat the egg yolks lightly until mixed. Dissolve the sugar in the water over gentle heat, bring to a boil and boil until the syrup spins a thread when a little is lifted on a spoon (230°F–234°F on a sugar thermometer). Gradually pour the hot syrup onto the egg yolks, beating constantly, and continue beating until the mixture is cool and thick and light. Cream the butter and gradually beat in the egg and sugar mixture. Flavor to taste with vanilla, orange or lemon rind, coffee or chocolate.

Note: if you like, flavor the butter cream with vanilla and use what you need; flavor the rest with coffee, use it; then flavor the remaining butter cream with chocolate. This last portion will blend all 3 flavors.

Butter Cream Frosting 2

For 1 cup quantity
1 cup unsalted butter
2 egg whites
1 cup confectioners' sugar

Method

Sift the confectioners' sugar onto a sheet of wax paper. Have ready a pan of simmering water. Beat the egg whites with a rotary or electric beater until frothy. Beat in the sifted sugar a teaspoon at a time. If beating by hand, set the bowl over hot water and continue beating until the mixture forms a tall peak when the beater is lifted; take from the heat and continue beating until cool. If using an electric beater, no heat is needed.

Cream the butter and beat the meringue mixture into it, a little at a time. Flavor and color as required.

Royal Icing

For 1 cup: sift $1\frac{3}{4}$ cups ($\frac{1}{2}$ lb) confectioners' sugar. Beat 1 egg white until frothy and beat in the confectioners' sugar, a tablespoon at a time. Continue beating until the mixture will stand in peaks. Beat in 1 teaspoon lemon juice.

Glacé Icing

For $\frac{3}{4}$ cup: sift 1 cup confectioners' sugar into a small bowl. Add $1–1\frac{1}{2}$ tablespoons water, stirring to make a smooth, fairly stiff, paste. Heat icing over pan of hot water until lukewarm – it should coat the back of a wooden spoon. If not, add a little more water or beat in more sifted confectioners' sugar. If you like, flavor with a little vanilla or a few drops of lemon juice.

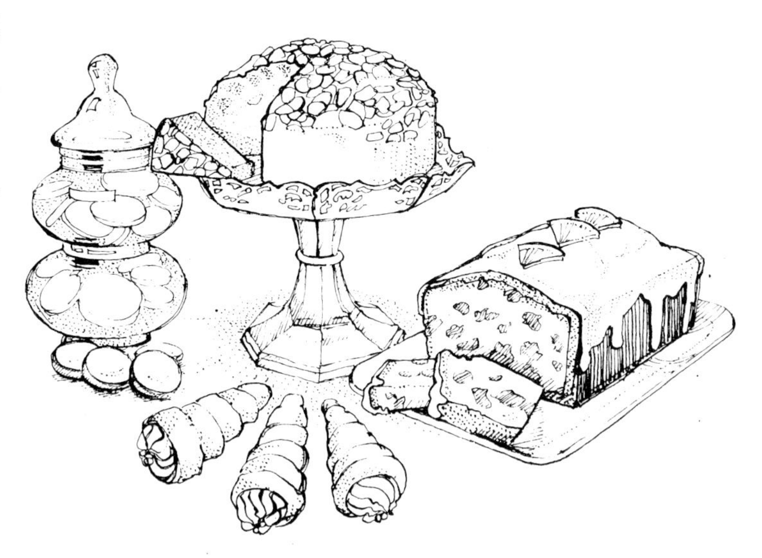

Fondant Icing

For 2 cup quantity
2 cups sugar
$\frac{3}{4}$ cup water
2 tablespoons corn syrup, or pinch of cream of tartar (dissolved in 1 teaspoon water)

Sugar thermometer

Fondant icing is often used in French pastries as it is sparkling white, glossy and pleasantly soft in texture. Fondant keeps well for 3–4 weeks in an airtight container.

Method

To make fondant: place sugar and water in a large saucepan over low heat and dissolve sugar slowly, following the rules for sugar boiling in the feature on candies in Volume 13. When dissolved, add corn syrup or dissolved cream of tartar, bring to a boil and boil steadily to the soft ball stage (240°F–242°F on a sugar thermometer). Take pan at once from heat, let bubbles subside and pour mixture slowly onto a dampened marble slab or into a dampened roasting pan.

Cool mixture slightly, add chosen flavoring and then pull batch together with a sugar scraper or metal spatula, taking the mixture from edge to center. Leave until fondant feels just warm to the touch. If using a roasting pan, turn out onto a Formica-type surface. Work vigorously with a sugar scraper or metal spatula in one hand and a wooden spoon in the other, turning and pulling it to the center until it becomes creamy – it will do this suddenly and become too stiff to work.

Then take a small piece of fondant at a time and work it with the fingers until smooth. Pack firm fondant in balls into a bowl or jar, cover tightly and let stand at least 1 hour and preferably 2–3 days to mellow before use.

Add food coloring, if liked, when melting fondant for icing.

To use Fondant for Icing

The consistency of finished fondant will vary from soft and pliable to stiff and almost hard, depending on the exact temperature to which it was boiled and the humidity of the atmosphere. Put the fondant in the top of a double boiler or in a bowl in a pan of hot water. Add a few spoons of sugar syrup (made by dissolving 1 cup sugar in $\frac{1}{2}$ cup water, bringing to a boil and boiling for 2 minutes). Heat the mixture until it is lukewarm, stirring until smooth and adding more sugar syrup as necessary so the warm fondant coats the back of a spoon. Add a few drops of food coloring, if you like.

Watchpoint: do not let fondant get too hot or it will lose its gloss. Add food coloring sparingly, if you want a pastel shade.

Set the cake to be coated on a wire rack over a tray or plate to catch the drips. Brush the cake with apricot jam glaze and let stand a few minutes to set. Pour the warm fondant all at once on top of the cake and spread it quickly with a metal spatula, working down the sides. Do not continue working the fondant on top of the cake after it starts to set or the finish will be rough. If necessary, the sides can be patched, then smoothed with a metal spatula dipped in hot water.

Pastry Cream

$1\frac{1}{2}$ cups milk
1 egg, separated
1 egg yolk
$\frac{1}{4}$ cup sugar
$1\frac{1}{2}$ tablespoons flour
1 tablespoon cornstarch

To flavor (optional)
1 vanilla bean or 1 teaspoon vanilla extract
2–3 squares (2–3 oz) semisweet chocolate
2–3 teaspoons dry instant coffee

Pastry cream is made with milk, thickened with egg yolks, flour and cornstarch. Softer and less rich than butter cream frosting, it does not keep as well.

This recipe gives a firm filling that holds its shape.

Method

Beat the egg yolks with the sugar until thick and light. Stir in the flour and cornstarch and just enough cold milk to make a smooth paste. If flavoring with chocolate, heat chocolate with remaining milk until melted, then bring just to a boil. If flavoring with vanilla bean, add bean to the milk and scald, cover and let stand 10–15 minutes to infuse. For other flavorings, simply scald the milk.

Stir the hot milk into the egg mixture, blend, return to the pan and stir constantly over gentle heat until boiling.

Watchpoint: make sure the pastry cream is smooth before letting it boil. If lumps form as it thickens take the pan from the heat and beat until smooth. Do not bring the pastry cream to a boil too quickly, or the mixture may curdle before it thickens.

Cook the cream gently for 2 minutes, stirring; if it is too stiff, add a little more milk. Remove the vanilla bean, if used.

Beat the egg white until it holds a stiff peak and fold in a little of the hot pastry cream, adding instant coffee or vanilla extract, if used. Fold this mixture into the remaining hot cream, pour into a bowl, cover and cool.

Chocolate Caraque

Grate 3 squares (3 oz) semisweet chocolate and melt on heatproof plate over a pan of hot water. Work with a metal spatula until smooth and spread thinly on marble slab or Formica-type surface. Let stand until nearly set. Hold a sharp, long knife or metal spatula almost at a right angle to the surface, and shave off long chocolate scrolls or flakes using a slight sideways sawing movement.

Caraque looks better when freshly made, but can be kept 1–2 days in airtight container.

Shave off chocolate scrolls, using a sideways sawing movement, for caraque

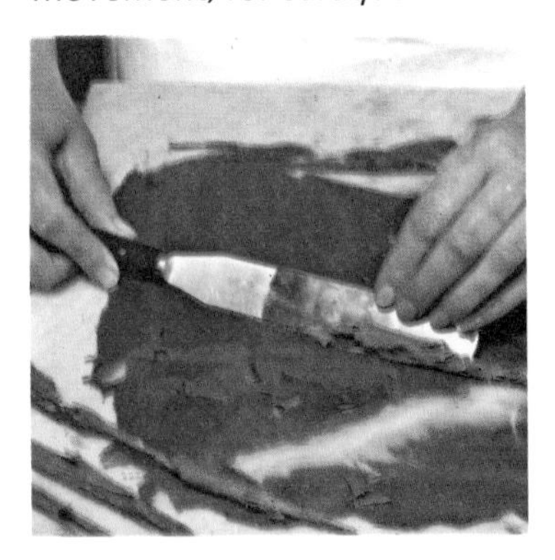

GATEAUX AND PASTRIES

Gâteau au Chocolat

$\frac{3}{4}$ cup flour
$\frac{1}{4}$ cup cocoa
$\frac{1}{4}$ teaspoon salt
3 tablespoons butter
4 eggs
$\frac{1}{2}$ cup sugar
$\frac{3}{4}$ cup quantity chocolate-flavored butter cream frosting 1
chocolate caraque
confectioners' sugar (for sprinkling)

8 inch springform pan

Method

Set oven at moderate (350°F). Grease cake pan and line base with wax paper circle, grease again and flour.

Sift flour several times with cocoa and salt. Warm butter in a bowl or pan over hot water until it is soft and pourable.

Watchpoint: take great care that the butter does not become hot or oily.

Break eggs into a large bowl, add the sugar and beat until mixed. Set bowl over a pan of boiling water so that it does not touch the water. Immediately take pan from heat and beat sugar and egg mixture 10–12 minutes or until light and thick enough to leave a ribbon trail when the beater is lifted. Take bowl from the pan and continue whisking 5 minutes or until mixture is cold. If using an electric beater, no heat is necessary. Fold in two-thirds of flour and cocoa mixture, then add cool butter with the remaining flour mixture and fold together as lightly as possible. Pour mixture into the prepared pan and bake in heated oven for 40 minutes or until the cake springs back when lightly pressed with a fingertip. Turn cake out to cool on a wire rack.

Make the chocolate-flavored butter cream frosting. When cake is cool, split it and sandwich with a thin layer of frosting. Reshape it and spread remaining frosting over top and sides. Lay largest scrolls of chocolate caraque on top of cake and press the smaller pieces around the edge. Cut 4 strips of paper $\frac{1}{2}$ inch wide and lay them across the cake parallel to each other and 1 inch apart. Sprinkle cake generously with confectioners' sugar, then carefully lift up paper strips leaving a striped pattern.

Arrange long scrolls of chocolate caraque on top of sponge cake for gâteau au chocolat

Quantity Terms

Terms like 1 cup quantity pastry or 1 cup quantity butter cream frosting refer to the amount obtained by using 1 cup of the principal ingredient at the top of the ingredient list, not 1 cup of prepared pastry dough or butter cream frosting.

Gâteau Moka (Coffee Cake)

4 egg quantity Génoise sponge cake
$\frac{3}{4}$ cup quantity coffee-flavored butter cream frosting 1

For decoration
$\frac{1}{2}$ cup whole blanched almonds, browned and ground, or finely chopped or slivered
confectioners' sugar (for sprinkling) – optional

9–10 inch moule à manqué or 8–9 inch springform pan; pastry bag and medium star tube

Method

Set oven at moderate (350°F) and prepare the mold or pan as in basic Génoise recipe. Make and bake cake and turn onto a wire rack to cool. Make coffee butter cream frosting.

Cut the cake in 2–3 layers, sandwich them with butter cream frosting and reshape cake. Spread top and sides with more frosting and press browned almonds around the sides with a metal spatula. Put remaining frosting into the pastry bag fitted with the star tube and decorate top of the cake with rosettes of frosting.

As an alternative: split cake in half and sandwich it with frosting. Spread top and sides with more frosting and press about $\frac{3}{4}$ cup browned slivered almonds over top and sides of cake. Sprinkle top with confectioners' sugar; pipe rosettes of frosting around top edge of cake.

Gâteau d'Isigny

4 egg quantity Génoise sponge cake, flavored with grated rind of $\frac{1}{2}$ lemon
$\frac{3}{4}$ cup quantity butter cream frosting 1 or 2
6 tablespoons raspberry purée or sieved raspberry jam
2 cup quantity white fondant icing

9–10 inch moule à manqué or 9 inch springform pan; paper decorating cone

Isigny, a village in Calvados, Normandy, is famous throughout France for its butter and cream.

Method

Set oven at moderate (350°F) and prepare cake pan as in basic Génoise recipe. Make and bake cake and turn it onto a wire rack to cool.

Make butter cream frosting and beat in raspberry purée or jam. When cake is cool, split and sandwich it together with about one-third of frosting. Reshape it; coat top and sides with remaining frosting. Chill cake until frosting is firm.

Melt the fondant icing taking care not to heat it more than lukewarm; pour over chilled cake, reserving a little; spread quickly with a metal spatula.

Watchpoint: the frosting must be thoroughly chilled or the icing will melt it.

Put reserved icing into paper decorating cone, trim tip and write Isigny across top of cake.

Gâteau aux Groseilles (Red Currant Cake)

3 egg quantity Génoise sponge cake
$\frac{1}{4}$ cup red currant jelly
$\frac{1}{4}$ cup apricot jam glaze
2 cup quantity white fondant icing
frosted red currants

9 inch round cake pan

Method

Set oven at moderate (350°F). Grease cake pan and line base with wax paper circle, grease again and flour. Make and bake cake and turn onto a wire rack to cool.

When cold, split the cake and sandwich it with red currant jelly. Reshape it, brush with warm apricot glaze and let it set. Melt the fondant icing, pour over the cake, spread it with a metal spatula and let stand until set. Transfer to a platter and decorate with frosted red currants.

As an alternative: make and bake cake, sandwich it with red currant jelly and coat it with apricot jam glaze as before. Melt $\frac{1}{4}$ cup red currant jelly in a small pan, put it into a paper decorating cone. Coat the cake with white fondant icing and, while it is still warm, pipe jelly (cut off tip of cone) in parallel straight lines across top of the cake. Run the point of a knife across the cake at right angles to jelly lines, first in one direction, then in another to marbleize the cake in a zigzag pattern.

Frosted Red Currants

Choose good sprigs of fresh red currants and wash and dry them thoroughly. Brush them lightly with egg white, beaten until frothy, and dip each sprig in granulated sugar. Let them stand on a wire rack or flat sieve for 2–3 hours to dry.

Gâteau St. Honoré

$\frac{1}{2}$ cup quantity French flan pastry
3–4 egg quantity choux pastry
1 egg, beaten to mix
$\frac{1}{4}$ cup sugar
2 tablespoons water
$1\frac{1}{4}$ cup quantity crème St. Honoré

For decoration
few candied cherries
few diamonds of candied angelica (optional)

Pastry bag and $\frac{3}{8}$ inch plain tube

Method

Make French flan pastry dough and chill thoroughly. Set oven at hot (400°F). Make the choux pastry dough.

Roll out French flan dough into a 7–8 inch circle one-eighth inch thick; trim edges neatly. Transfer the round to a baking sheet, prick dough well and brush a $\frac{1}{2}$ inch wide band around the edge with beaten egg.

Put choux dough into pastry bag fitted with the plain tube and make a circle around the edge of the flan dough, using about one-third of the choux dough. Brush this choux circle with beaten egg and bake flan in heated oven for about 20 minutes or until choux pastry is puffed and brown and flan pastry is pale golden. Cool slightly, then transfer to a platter.

On a dampened baking sheet pipe remaining choux dough in small mounds about the size of a walnut. Brush tops with beaten egg and bake in heated oven for 12–15 minutes or until the puffs are crisp and brown. Transfer to a wire rack, pierce a hole in the side to release steam and let cool.

Dissolve the sugar in the water, bring to a boil and boil steadily until the syrup just looks pale golden (310°F on a sugar thermometer). Set the base of the pan in cold water to stop syrup cooking further, quickly dip each choux puff into the sugar syrup and place them touching each other around the edge of the flan, on top of the choux pastry circle.

Pile crème St. Honoré in the center of the gâteau and decorate choux puffs with candied cherries and angelica.

Crème St. Honoré

$1\frac{1}{4}$ cups milk
4 egg yolks
$\frac{1}{2}$ cup sugar
2 tablespoons flour
vanilla bean
6 egg whites

Method

Beat egg yolks and sugar until thick and light. Stir in flour and enough cold milk to make a smooth paste. Scald remaining milk with vanilla bean, cover and let stand 10 minutes to infuse. Discard bean.

Gradually pour hot milk into egg mixture, blend and return to pan. Bring to a boil over low heat, stirring constantly. Simmer 1–2 minutes and remove from heat. Whip egg whites until they hold a stiff peak and fold about one-quarter into the hot cream.

Watchpoint: the heat of the cream is enough to cook the egg whites slightly and 'set' them. Fold in remaining egg whites. Transfer cream to a bowl to cool.

Gâteau d'Ananas (Pineapple Cake)

3 egg quantity Génoise sponge cake
$\frac{1}{2}$ cup quantity butter cream frosting 2, flavored with lemon juice or kirsch
$\frac{1}{4}$ cup apricot jam glaze
candied pineapple
2 cup quantity white fondant icing

8–9 inch moule à manqué or 7–8 inch springform pan

Method

Set the oven at moderate (350°F) and prepare cake pan as in basic Génoise recipe. Make and bake cake and turn onto a wire rack to cool.

Make butter cream frosting and flavor with lemon juice or kirsch. When the cake is cool, split and sandwich it with all the butter cream frosting. Reshape it and brush top and sides with warm apricot jam glaze. Let stand to set, then arrange overlapping slices of candied pineapple on top of the cake.

Melt the fondant icing – it should be slightly thinner than the usual coating consistency so the candied pineapple shows through the icing. Pour the fondant icing over the cake, spread quickly with a metal spatula and let stand until set.

Candied Pineapple

Drain a small can ($8\frac{1}{2}$ oz) pineapple slices, reserve juice and halve each slice to form 2 thin rounds.

In a large skillet or frying pan heat $\frac{1}{2}$ cup reserved juice with 2 tablespoons sugar until sugar is dissolved. Add pineapple slices and simmer gently for 10–15 minutes or until transparent, turning from time to time. If too hot, syrup will caramelize.

Drain slices and let dry in an airy place before use. With fresh pineapple use water for juice and add $\frac{1}{2}$ cup sugar.

Quantity Terms

Terms like 1 cup quantity pastry or 1 cup quantity butter cream frosting refer to the amount obtained by using 1 cup of the principal ingredient at the top of the ingredient list, not 1 cup of prepared pastry dough or butter cream frosting.

Classic French gâteaux are from left: gâteau aux groseilles (with frosted red currants), gâteau moka, and gâteau St. Honoré, with its traditional circle of choux puffs

Gâteau Flamande, made with French flan pastry and frangipane, is decorated with glacé icing and candied cherries

Gâteau Flamande

- 1 cup quantity French flan pastry
- $\frac{1}{2}$ cup candied cherries
- 2–3 tablespoons kirsch
- 1 cup quantity frangipane, flavored with 1 tablespoon kirsch
- granulated sugar (for dipping)

For decoration
- $\frac{1}{2}$ cup shredded almonds
- $\frac{3}{4}$ cup quantity thick glacé icing

8 inch diameter flan ring

Method

Make French flan pastry dough and chill 1 hour. Slice cherries, reserving 8–10 for decoration, add the kirsch, cover and let macerate. Set oven at moderately hot (375°F). Roll out dough, line flan ring and chill.

Make the frangipane. Spread sliced cherries on the bottom of the flan shell, cover with frangipane and spread the almonds on top. Bake gâteau in heated oven for 40–45 minutes or until a skewer inserted in the center comes out clean. Cool slightly, remove the flan ring and transfer gâteau to a wire rack to cool completely. Then coat the top with glacé icing. Dip reserved candied cherries in sugar and arrange them around the edge.

Gâteau Chinois à l'Orange

- 1 cup flour
- pinch of salt
- 4 eggs
- $\frac{3}{4}$ cup sugar
- few slices of candied ginger or 1–2 candied orange slices (for decoration)

For filling
- 5–6 sugar cubes
- 2 oranges
- $1\frac{1}{2}$ cups heavy cream, stiffly whipped
- $\frac{1}{4}$ cup candied ginger

Pastry bag and star tube

Method

Grease 3 baking sheets, sprinkle them with flour and discard the excess. Mark an 8-inch circle on each sheet, using a plate or pan lid as guide. Set the oven at moderately hot (375°F).

Sift the flour with the salt. In a bowl beat the eggs until mixed and gradually beat in the sugar. Set the bowl over a pan of boiling water, take the pan from the heat and beat until the mixture is thick enough to leave a ribbon trail when the whisk is lifted. Take from the heat and continue beating until cool. If using an electric beater, no heat is necessary.

Fold in the flour in 3 batches, using a metal spoon. Spread one-sixth of the mixture into an 8-inch circle on each baking sheet and bake in the heated oven for 5–8 minutes or until the cakes are lightly browned. When the mixture is still warm, trim neatly with a knife to an 8-inch round and transfer them to a wire rack to cool. Cool the baking sheets, grease and flour them again and cook the remaining mixture in the same way, making 3 more rounds.

To make the filling: rub the sugar cubes over the oranges to remove all the zest (oil), then pound the sugar to a syrup with a little orange juice. Beat the syrup into the stiffly whipped cream, reserving about $\frac{1}{2}$ cup for decoration.

Pour boiling water over the ginger, let stand 10 minutes to soften it, then drain well on paper towels and chop it.

Sandwich the cake with orange-flavored cream, piling one layer of cake on another and sprinkling each layer of cream with chopped ginger. Coat the sides of the cake with the remaining orange cream.

Put the reserved cream into a pastry bag fitted with a star tube and decorate the top of the cake with rosettes. Top each rosette with a piece of candied ginger or candied orange peel.

Gateau Chinois à l'orange, cut to show the layer sandwiched with the orange-flavored cream

Gâteau aux fraises – Japonais rounds are sandwiched with butter cream frosting flavored with fresh strawberry purée and kirsch

Gâteau aux Fraises

3 egg quantity Génoise sponge cake
$\frac{1}{2}$ cup slivered almonds, browned and chopped

For Japonais mixture
1 cup whole blanched almonds, ground
$\frac{3}{4}$ cup sugar
3 egg whites
1 cup quantity butter cream frosting 1 or 2
1 pint fresh strawberries, hulled
1 tablespoon kirsch
few drops of pink food coloring

9–10 inch moule à manqué or springform pan; pastry bag and small star tube

Method

Set oven at moderate (350°F) and prepare the cake pan as in the basic Génoise recipe. Make and bake the cake and turn it onto a wire rack to cool.

To make the Japonais mixture: set oven at low (300°F) and line 2 baking sheets with silicone paper. Mark a 9–10 inch circle on each sheet. Work ground almonds and sugar together through a coarse sieve. Stiffly whip the egg whites and fold in the almond mixture. Spread the mixture on the prepared baking sheets in two 9–10 inch circles and bake in the heated oven for 25–30 minutes or until the rounds are crisp and very lightly browned. Trim the rounds neatly with a knife while still hot, let cool to tepid, then peel off the paper and transfer to a wire rack to cool completely.

Make the butter cream frosting. Work the strawberries through a sieve or purée them in a blender and beat them gradually into the butter cream frosting.

Watchpoint: if the purée is added too quickly or the butter cream frosting is cold, it will separate.

Beat in the kirsch and a few drops of coloring to tint the frosting a clear pink.

When the cake is cool, split and sandwich it together with a very little of the frosting. Spread a thin layer of frosting on one Japonais round, set the cake on top, spread it thinly with frosting and cover it with the second Japonais round.

Coat the top and sides of the cake with half the remaining frosting and press browned chopped almonds around the lower part of the sides. Put the remaining frosting into a pastry bag fitted with a small star tube and decorate the cake with bands and rosettes of frosting.

Gâteau Cendrillon (Cinderella Cake)

3-egg quantity Génoise sponge cake
2 teaspoons dry instant coffee dissolved in a little water
$\frac{3}{4}$ cup quantity coffee butter cream frosting 1 or 2
$\frac{1}{4}$ cup apricot jam glaze
2 cup quantity coffee-flavored fondant icing
8–10 hazelnuts, browned, or 4–5 almonds, browned and split lengthwise

8–9 inch moule à manqué or 8 inch springform pan; pastry bag and star tube

Method

Set oven at moderate (350°F). Grease and flour the cake pan, lining the base with a circle of wax paper.

Make the Génoise batter, adding the dissolved coffee to the eggs and sugar before beating. Bake the cake and turn onto a wire rack to cool.

Make the coffee butter cream frosting. When the cake is cool, split it and sandwich it with about one-third of the butter cream frosting. Reshape the cake, brush the top and sides with melted apricot jam glaze and let stand until set.

Melt the fondant icing and add dry instant coffee to taste. Pour fondant over the cake, spread it quickly with a metal spatula and let stand until set. Fill the remaining butter cream frosting into the pastry bag fitted with the star tube and decorate the top edge of the cake with 8–10 rosettes of frosting. Top each rosette with a browned hazelnut or split almond.

Gâteau Praliné

4-egg quantity Génoise sponge cake
$\frac{3}{4}$ cup quantity butter cream frosting 1 or 2
$\frac{1}{4}$ cup apricot jam glaze
$\frac{1}{2}$ cup whole blanched almonds, browned and ground

For praline
$\frac{1}{2}$ cup sugar
$\frac{1}{2}$ cup whole unblanched almonds

9–10 inch moule à manqué or 9 inch springform pan

Method

Set oven at moderate (350°F) and prepare the cake pan as in basic Génoise recipe.

Make and bake the cake and turn out on a wire rack to cool.

To make the praline: put the almonds and sugar in a pan and cook slowly to a deep brown, stirring with a metal spoon until the sugar begins to brown. Turn praline onto an oiled baking sheet or pan to cool. When cold and brittle, grind in a rotary cheese grater or in the blender and sieve to obtain a fine powder.

Make the butter cream frosting and beat in the praline powder. When the cake is cold split it and sandwich it with all the praline butter cream. Reshape and brush the top and sides with well reduced apricot jam glaze. Let set, then cover the cake with browned ground almonds, pressing them on well with a metal spatula.

Gâteau au caramel is decorated with rosettes of Chantilly cream and crushed caramel

Gâteau au Caramel

4-egg quantity Génoise sponge cake flavored with grated rind of $\frac{1}{2}$ lemon
Chantilly cream made with $1\frac{1}{2}$ cups heavy cream, stiffly whipped and flavored with $1-1\frac{1}{2}$ tablespoons sugar and 1 teaspoon vanilla
$\frac{1}{3}$ cup slivered almonds, browned and finely chopped

For caramel
$1\frac{1}{2}$ cups sugar
1 cup water

11 X 16 inch jelly roll pan; pastry bag and small star tube

Method

Set the oven at moderate (350°F) and prepare cake pan as in basic Génoise recipe. Make cake and bake 12–15 minutes or until lightly browned. Let cool slightly, then turn out on a wire rack to cool completely.

To make the caramel: oil a baking sheet or roasting pan. Heat the sugar with the water until dissolved, bring to a boil and boil steadily without stirring to a rich brown caramel.

Watchpoint: if the caramel is pale, the gâteau will taste too sweet.

Take the pan from the heat, dip the base in cold water to stop cooking and pour the caramel onto the prepared baking sheet or roasting pan. Leave until cold and hard. Crack the caramel into pieces, then grind three-quarters of it in a rotary cheese grater or work it in a blender to a fine powder. Coarsely crush the remaining caramel in a mortar and pestle or with the end of a rolling pin in a bowl.

Trim the edges of the cake; cut it in half lengthwise and in thirds crosswise to make six 5-inch squares.

Using about half the Chantilly cream, sandwich the cake with cream, piling the layers of cake one on top of another. Sprinkle each layer of cream with powdered caramel. Cover the top and sides of the cake with cream, reserving a little for decoration.

Press the finely chopped browned nuts around the sides of the cake. Put the remaining Chantilly cream into a pastry bag fitted with a small star tube and decorate the top of the cake with rosettes. Sprinkle the top with crushed caramel.

PASTRIES

Printaniers

4-egg quantity Génoise sponge cake
2 cup quantity butter cream frosting 2

For flavoring and coloring
vanilla
dissolved instant coffee
little fresh strawberry purée (see gâteau aux fraises, page 95) or sieved strawberry jam
red food coloring
2 cup quantity fondant icing

11 X 16 inch jelly roll pan; pastry bag and $\frac{5}{8}$ inch plain tube

Makes about 35 printaniers.

Method

Set the oven at moderately hot (375°F) and grease and flour the cake pan.

Make the Génoise batter and bake in the heated oven for 12–15 minutes or until the cake springs back when lightly pressed with a fingertip. Turn out on a wire rack to cool.

Make the butter cream frosting and flavor a little of it with vanilla. Split the cool cake, sandwich it with the vanilla-flavored butter cream frosting, trim the edges and cut the cake in 7 long strips, each about $1\frac{1}{2}$ inches wide. Divide the remaining butter cream frosting in 3 portions; flavor one with vanilla, another with coffee and the third with strawberry purée or jam, adding a few drops of coloring to make it a delicate pink.

Fill the vanilla butter cream frosting into the pastry bag fitted with the plain tube and pipe a line of frosting along one side on the top of each strip of cake. Pipe a line of coffee butter cream frosting beside it and top them with a line of strawberry butter cream frosting, piped down the middle. Chill until the frosting is firm.

Watchpoint: be sure the frosting is very cold or the icing will melt when the fondant icing is poured over.

Melt the fondant icing but do not let it become more than lukewarm. Coat the strips of cake with icing and when set, cut them diagonally into sections about 3 inches long and $\frac{3}{4}$ inch wide exposing the colored butter cream frosting.

Quantity Terms

Terms like 1 cup quantity pastry or 1 cup quantity butter cream frosting refer to the amount obtained by using 1 cup of the principal ingredient at the top of the ingredient list, not 1 cup of prepared pastry dough or butter cream frosting.

French pastries include from left: chocolatines, Madeleines, tartelettes amandines, bâteaux de miel, mirlitons, more bâteaux and tartelettes, gâteaux St. André and chocolatines

Quantity Terms

Terms like 1 cup quantity pastry or 1 cup quantity butter cream frosting refer to the amount obtained by using 1 cup of the principal ingredient at the top of the ingredient list, not 1 cup of prepared pastry dough or butter cream frosting.

Madeleines

2 large eggs
$\frac{1}{2}$ cup cake flour
$\frac{1}{4}$ cup sugar
2 teaspoons honey
1 teaspoon orange flower water or 1 tablespoon rum
$\frac{1}{4}$ cup butter, softened until it pours easily but is not oily

12–18 madeleine molds; pastry bag and $\frac{1}{2}$ inch plain tube (optional)

Makes 12–18 Madeleines.

Method

Set oven at moderately hot (375°F). Brush the molds thickly with melted butter, chill until firm, then brush again.

Sift the flour. Put eggs with the sugar, honey and orange flower water or rum in a bowl and beat 12–15 minutes until the mixture is light and leaves a thick ribbon trail when the beater is lifted.

Watchpoint: for this recipe do not beat over hot water if using a rotary beater.

Fold in two-thirds of the sifted flour, pour in the softened butter and fold together carefully with the remaining flour. Put the mixture into pastry bag fitted with the plain tube and fill the prepared pans two-thirds full with batter; or use a spoon to fill the pans.

Bake in heated oven for about 10 minutes or until the Madeleines are delicately browned. Transfer them to a wire rack to cool.

Madeleines were acclaimed by Marcel Proust – whose mother always served him some at tea. Today they are found throughout France and are always baked in the characteristic shell-shaped mold. They may be flavored with honey, orange or lemon rind, orange flower water or rum and they appear deceptively simple but the right buttery, crumbling texture of these little sponge cakes is hard to achieve.

Tartelettes Amandines (Almond Tartlets)

1 cup quantity French flan pastry
$\frac{1}{2}$ cup quantity frangipane
$\frac{1}{2}$ cup shredded almonds
$\frac{1}{4}$ cup apricot jam or red currant jelly glaze
2 tablespoons ground almonds (for decoration)

12 tartlet pans; pastry bag and $\frac{1}{2}$ inch plain tube (optional)

It is easier to fill the tartlets with the frangipane if it is put in using a pastry bag fitted with a $\frac{1}{2}$ inch plain tube.

Method

Make French flan pastry dough and chill 1 hour. Set oven at moderately hot (375°F).

Line dough into the pans. Make the frangipane, fill each pastry shell and sprinkle the tops with shredded almonds. Bake in the heated oven for 12–15 minutes or until the frangipane and almonds are lightly browned.

Transfer the tartlets to a wire rack to cool, brush the tops with melted glaze and decorate the edges with a thin border of ground almonds.

Bâteaux de Miel (Almond and Honey Cakes)

1 cup quantity French flan pastry

For filling
$\frac{3}{4}$ cup whole blanched almonds, ground
1 tablespoon honey
6 tablespoons unsalted butter
6 tablespoons sugar
1–2 teaspoons dry instant coffee dissolved in water
1 cup quantity fondant icing, flavored with dissolved instant coffee to taste

12–16 boat molds

Method

Make French flan pastry dough and chill 1 hour. Set oven at moderately hot (375°F). Line molds with dough and bake blind in heated oven for 5–7 minutes or until pale golden. Unmold them and let stand on a wire rack to cool.

To make filling: cream butter, gradually add sugar and beat until soft and light. Stir in ground almonds and honey with instant coffee to taste. Fill pastry cases with the almond and honey mixture, piling it high, then shaping it to an inverted 'V' with the blade of a knife. Chill until firm.

Melt the fondant icing and add instant coffee to taste. Coat the bâteaux with icing, trimming the edges with the blade of a knife to give a neat finish.

Gâteaux St. André

1 cup quantity French flan pastry

For apple marmelade
3 medium tart apples with skins wiped, quartered and cored
1 tablespoon butter
strip of lemon rind
6–8 tablespoons sugar

For royal icing
1 cup confectioners' sugar
1 egg white
pinch of flour

12 boat molds

Method

Make French flan pastry dough and chill 1 hour. Set oven at moderately hot (375°F).

To make apple marmelade: thickly butter a heavy casserole, add apples with the lemon rind, cover with buttered brown paper and the lid, and cook gently until soft, stirring occasionally. Remove the lemon rind, work apples through a sieve or purée in a blender. Return purée to the pan with sugar to taste and cook rapidly on top of the stove, or in heated oven, until the mixture is stiff but still falls easily from a spoon. Chill it. When cold it should be stiff enough to hold a shape.

Line molds with dough, reserving the trimmings for decoration. Fill them with chilled apple marmelade.

To make the royal icing: sift confectioners' sugar into a bowl. Beat egg white until frothy and beat in the confectioners' sugar, 1 tablespoon at a time. Add flour and continue beating until the mixture will stand in peaks.

Cover the apple marmelade with royal icing and place 2 bands of pastry $\frac{1}{4}$ inch wide on top to form a diagonal cross (St. Andrew's Cross). Press the ends of the cross against the edges of the pastry shell. Bake in heated oven for 10–12 minutes or until pastry and icing are lightly browned. Cool the gâteaux to lukewarm before removing from the molds.

Mirlitons

1 cup quantity French flan pastry
2–3 tablespoons apricot jam

For filling
10–12 large macaroons
2 eggs
$\frac{1}{3}$ cup sugar
$\frac{1}{2}$ teaspoon vanilla

To finish
15–18 whole blanched almonds, halved lengthwise
confectioners' sugar (for sprinkling)

10–12 tartlet pans

Mirlitons are a specialty of the town of Rouen in France.

Method

Make French flan pastry dough and chill 1 hour. Set oven at low (300°F).

Line pans with dough, place a little apricot jam in each one.

To prepare filling: break macaroons in small pieces and bake in heated oven for 10–15 minutes until quite dry. Crush them with a rolling pin and work them through a sieve or in a blender – there should be 1 cup of powdered macaroons.

Beat the eggs with the sugar in a bowl until light and thick enough to leave a ribbon trail when the beater is lifted.

Watchpoint: for this recipe do not beat over hot water if using a rotary beater.

Fold in powdered macaroons with the vanilla. Fill pastry shells with the mixture, top each with 3 almond halves and sprinkle generously with confectioners' sugar. Bake in heated oven for about 15 minutes or until the mirlitons are lightly browned.

Galettes Bretonnaise

1 cup flour
$\frac{1}{4}$ cup butter
$\frac{1}{2}$ cup sugar
1 small egg
$\frac{1}{2}$ teaspoon vanilla or grated rind of $\frac{1}{2}$ lemon
1 cup currants
little beaten egg (for glaze)

$2\frac{1}{2}$–3 inch cookie cutter

Makes about 18 cookies.

Method

Make dough as for French flan pastry, adding vanilla or lemon rind and working in currants when the dough is smooth. Chill 1 hour.

Set oven at moderate (350°F). Lightly grease a baking sheet. Roll out dough to $\frac{3}{4}$ inch thickness and cut out rounds with cookie cutter. Set rounds on prepared baking sheet, brush with beaten egg and bake in heated oven 8–10 minutes or until cookies are lightly browned. Cool on a wire rack.

Galettes (flat round cakes) are usually sweet gâteaux or cookies. They can also be savory mixtures turned out from flat round molds.

Chocolatines

4–egg quantity Génoise sponge cake
$1\frac{1}{2}$ cup quantity chocolate-flavored butter cream frosting 1
1 cup whole blanched almonds, browned and ground or finely chopped

8 inch square cake pan; pastry bag and small star tube

Makes 16 chocolatines.

Method

Set oven at moderate (350°F) and prepare cake pan as in basic Génoise recipe. Make and bake cake; cool on a wire rack.

Make chocolate-flavored butter cream frosting. When cake is cool, split and sandwich with some of the frosting. Trim cake; cut into 2 inch squares. Spread top and sides of each square with frosting, reserving about one-quarter. Press almonds around sides, using a metal spatula.

Put remaining frosting into a pastry bag fitted with a star tube and decorate the tops of the cakes with rosettes.

Alternative decoration: bake cake, sandwich and cut into 2-inch squares as above. Spread top and sides with the frosting and decorate top with rosettes. Melt 8 squares (8 oz) semisweet chocolate on a heatproof plate over pan of hot water, let cool to tepid, spread in one-eighth inch layer on 16 X 16 inch square of wax paper. When starting to set, mark chocolate into 64 2-inch squares and chill until set. Carefully peel squares off paper and press them around sides of chocolatines.

French gâteaux and pastries

Chocolatines are decorated with rosettes of chocolate-flavored butter cream frosting

From left to right, this selection of pastries and cookies shows: fourées au miel, galettes Suisse and Vénitiennes

Fourées au Miel
(Honey Cookies)

1 cup quantity French flan pastry
2–3 tablespoons thick honey
$\frac{1}{2}$ cup mixed candied fruits, finely chopped
1 tablespoon rum
confectioners' sugar (for sprinkling)

2 inch cookie cutter

This recipe is a good way to use up trimmings of French flan pastry dough; makes 9–12 cookies.

Method

If not using trimmings, make French flan pastry dough and chill for 1 hour.

Mix candied fruits with the rum, cover and let macerate 30 minutes. Work fruit mixture into dough and chill again.

Set oven at moderately hot (375°F); grease a baking sheet.

Roll out dough about $\frac{1}{4}$ inch thick on a floured board. Cut into rounds with the cookie cutter, set them on prepared baking sheet and bake in heated oven for 10–12 minutes or until a pale golden color. Cool on a wire rack. Sandwich cookies with honey and sprinkle tops with confectioners' sugar.

Bâteaux Célestins
(Heavenly Cakes)

1 cup quantity French flan pastry
2 tablespoons apricot jam
1 egg quantity Madeleine batter (see page 98)
grated rind of 1 orange
$\frac{1}{4}$ cup apricot jam glaze
1 cup quantity fondant or $\frac{3}{4}$ cup glacé icing, flavored with orange juice to taste

12–16 boat molds; pastry bag and $\frac{1}{2}$ inch plain tube (optional)

Method

Make French flan pastry dough and chill 1 hour. Set the oven at moderately hot (375°F).

Line molds with dough and put a little apricot jam in each. Make the Madeleine batter, substituting orange rind for the orange flower water or rum, and fill the pastry boats, preferably using pastry bag fitted with the plain tube.

Bake the cakes in heated oven for 10–15 minutes or until risen and lightly browned. Turn them upside down on a wire rack to cool.

Brush the tops of cakes with melted apricot glaze; let stand to set. Melt fondant icing with orange juice instead of sugar syrup or make glacé icing with orange juice instead of water. Coat each cake with icing, trim the sides with the blade of a knife to give a neat finish.

Fanchonnettes à la Vanille

1 cup quantity French flan pastry
$\frac{3}{4}$ cup quantity vanilla-flavored pastry cream

For meringue
2 egg whites
$\frac{1}{2}$ cup sugar

To finish
confectioners' sugar (for sprinkling)
1 tablespoon red currant jelly

10–12 tartlet pans; pastry bag and $\frac{1}{2}$ inch plain tube

Fanchonnettes are named for the heroine of a French play of that name written in 1800.

Method

Make French flan pastry dough and chill 1 hour. Set the oven at moderate (350°F). Make the pastry cream and cool.

Line pans with dough, fill with pastry cream level with the tops and bake in heated oven for 10–12 minutes or until the pastry is lightly browned.

To make meringue: stiffly beat the egg whites, add 1 tablespoon sugar and beat until the mixture is glossy. Fold in the remaining sugar. Put the meringue into pastry bag fitted with the plain tube. Pipe a circle of meringue in the center of each tartlet and decorate edge with small rounds of meringue. Sprinkle with confectioners' sugar, turn the oven to low (300°F) and continue baking 15 minutes or until meringue is firm and pale golden.

Cool the tartlets on a wire rack, sprinkle them with confectioners' sugar, decorate the centers with a little red currant jelly.

Vénitiennes
(Venetian Cookies)

1 cup quantity French flan pastry
1 cup quantity royal icing
2 tablespoons thick apricot jam glaze

Paper decorating cone

Makes 18–20 cookies.

Method

Make French flan pastry dough; chill 1 hour. Set oven at moderately hot (375°F). Roll out dough to a rectangle one-eighth inch thick. Spread royal icing smoothly over dough with a floured metal spatula; cut into 2 inch squares with a floured knife. Set cookies a little apart on an ungreased baking sheet; they may spread slightly in cooking.

Put apricot jam glaze into decorating cone and trim the tip. Pipe a star pattern of fine lines on each cookie. Bake in heated oven for 10–12 minutes or until the pastry is lightly browned and the icing is crisp.

Quantity Terms

Terms like 1 cup quantity pastry or 1 cup quantity butter cream frosting refer to the amount obtained by using 1 cup of the principal ingredient at the top of the ingredient list, not 1 cup of prepared pastry dough or butter cream frosting.

Galettes Suisse

For almond pastry
1 cup whole blanched almonds, ground
1 cup flour
$\frac{1}{2}$ cup sugar
3 tablespoons butter
3 egg yolks or 1 whole egg
1 teaspoon vanilla
pinch of salt

To finish
little beaten egg (for glaze)
$\frac{1}{4}$ cup slivered almonds
granulated sugar (for sprinkling)

2$\frac{1}{2}$–3 inch cookie cutter

Makes 20 cookies.

Method

Make almond pastry dough as for French flan pastry, adding ground almonds to the flour, and chill 1 hour. Set oven at moderate (350°F) and lightly grease a baking sheet. Roll out dough about $\frac{1}{4}$ inch thick on a lightly floured board and cut out rounds with a cookie cutter. Place rounds on prepared baking sheet and brush with beaten egg. Scatter with slivered almonds, sprinkle with sugar and bake in heated oven 8–10 minutes or until a pale golden color.

Quantity Terms

Terms like 1 cup quantity pastry or 1 cup quantity butter cream frosting refer to the amount obtained by using 1 cup of the principal ingredient at the top of the ingredient list, not 1 cup of prepared pastry dough or butter cream frosting.

Croissants de Provence

1 cup whole blanched almonds, ground
$\frac{1}{2}$ cup sugar
1 tablespoon very thick apricot jam glaze
$\frac{1}{2}$ teaspoon vanilla
1 large egg white
1 egg, beaten to mix
$\frac{1}{2}$ cup whole blanched almonds, chopped

To finish
1 tablespoon sugar, dissolved in 2 tablespoons milk

Makes 12 crescents.

Method

Set oven at moderate (350°F). Pound the ground almonds in a mortar and pestle or with the end of a rolling pin in a bowl, adding the sugar gradually. Work in apricot jam glaze and vanilla and add the egg white a little at a time, using only enough to make a paste that can be rolled with the hand.

Divide the mixture into balls the size of a large walnut and roll them with your hand on a floured board to finger-sized cylinders. Brush with beaten egg and roll in chopped almonds, making sure they are completely coated with nuts.

Bend the rolls into crescents and place on foil or silicone paper on a baking sheet. Brush again with beaten egg and bake in heated oven for 10 minutes or until lightly browned. Take baking sheet from oven and at once pull off sheet of paper with all crescents on it. Brush them while still hot with sweetened milk.

Gaufrettes Viennoise (Viennese Wafers)

For almond pastry
$\frac{3}{4}$ cup whole blanched almonds, ground
2 cups flour
pinch of salt
$\frac{3}{4}$ cup butter
6 tablespoons sugar
1 egg

To decorate
$\frac{1}{2}$ cup quantity royal icing
2–3 tablespoons red currant jelly or raspberry jam

Paper decorating cone

Makes 18 gaufrettes.

Method

Make dough as for French flan pastry, adding almonds with the flour, and chill 1 hour.

Set oven at moderately hot (375°F). Roll out dough to a rectangle one-eighth inch thick and place on an ungreased baking sheet. Trim edges with a floured knife, then cut the dough into 2 inch squares.

Put royal icing into a paper decorating cone and trim tip of cone. Decorate half the squares with a fine lattice pattern of royal icing.

Bake the gaufrettes in heated oven for 7–8 minutes or until pale golden. Cool on a wire rack. When cool, spread each plain square with red currant jelly or raspberry jam and place a decorated square on top.

Galettes Nantaise

For almond pastry
$\frac{1}{2}$ cup whole blanched almonds, ground
1 cup flour
pinch of salt
$\frac{1}{4}$ cup butter
$\frac{1}{4}$ cup sugar
2 egg yolks

To finish
little beaten egg (for glaze)
1 tablespoon ground almonds
granulated sugar (for sprinkling)

2$\frac{1}{2}$–3 inch fluted cookie cutter

Nantes, in northwest France, is renowned for its cookies. This recipe makes 18–20 galettes.

Method

Make almond pastry dough in the same way as French flan pastry, adding the ground almonds to the flour, and chill 1 hour.

Set oven at moderately hot (375°F). Lightly grease a baking sheet. Roll out dough about $\frac{1}{4}$ inch thick on a lightly floured board and cut into rounds with cookie cutter.

Place rounds on prepared baking sheet; brush with beaten egg. Mark tops of rounds into checkerboard squares with the prongs of a fork, put a pinch of ground almonds in the center of each, and sprinkle generously with sugar. Bake in heated oven 7–8 minutes or until pale golden. Cool on a wire rack.

French gâteaux and pastries

From left to right pastries shown are: croissants de Provence, gaufrettes Viennoise and galettes Nantaise

Suprêmes de poulet Villeroi – stuffed chicken suprêmes are arranged inside a border of duchesse potatoes and coated with sauce *(recipe is on page 109)*

AN ELEGANT DINNER

Serve your guests in style with a menu of classic French dishes – fillets of sole meunière, chicken suprêmes stuffed with mushrooms and cream, and a rich Génoise sponge cake layered with butter cream frosting and covered with coffee-flavored glacé icing.

With the splendid simplicity of this appetizer an equally straightforward white wine seems in order. The whites from Burgundy have a quality all their own. Choose one from the Mâconnais in southern Burgundy; from a top shipper like Louis Latour they represent excellent value. America's nearest equivalent is the Pinot Blanc, at its best from California's Livermore Valley. A light red wine from Burgundy such as a Santenay would suit the boned chicken breasts, or try a California Pinot St. George.

Fillets of Sole Meunière

Suprêmes de Poulet Villeroi
(Chicken Suprêmes Villeroi)

Buttered Green Beans or Broccoli

Gâteau au Café with
Fruits Rafraîchis

White wine for fish – Mâcon Blanc (Côte Mâconnais)
or Pinot Blanc (California)
Red wine for chicken – Santenay (Côte de Beaune)
or Pinot St. George (California)

TIMETABLE

Day before
Cut circles of foil for the chicken. Make and bake Génoise sponge cake for gâteau. Store in airtight container. Make butter cream frosting and apricot jam glaze and keep covered. Make sugar syrup for fruit and for glacé icing and store in screwtop jars.
Cut suprêmes from chickens, if necessary, and keep covered in refrigerator.
Prepare duxelles stuffing, keep covered in a bowl in refrigerator.
Make chicken stock from giblets and carcass bones and keep covered in refrigerator.

Morning
Split and fill cake, glaze, ice and decorate with butter cream frosting. Prepare fruit for salad, pour over the syrup, cover and refrigerate.
Split and stuff suprêmes, sprinkle with wine, wrap 'en papillote' in the foil and place on baking sheet ready for cooking. Make velouté sauce for chicken but do not add liaison.
Prepare green beans or broccoli. Wash fish fillets and pat dry.

Assemble ingredients for final cooking from 6:45 for dinner around 8 p.m.

Order of Work
6:45
Set oven at moderate (350°F). Arrange gâteau au café on a serving platter.
7:00
Put suprêmes of chicken in oven.
Begin cooking potatoes.
Fry bacon for sole, drain and keep warm.
7:20
Cook green beans or broccoli.
Drain potatoes, make duchesse potatoes, pipe them onto gratin dish and brown in the oven.
7:45
Turn oven to low.
Coat the fish fillets with seasoned flour, fry, arrange on platter with bacon and keep warm.
Reheat velouté sauce for chicken, add liaison and keep hot in a water bath.
Arrange chicken in gratin dish, do not add the sauce, cover and keep warm.
8:00
Prepare butter sauce for fish, pour it over the fillets and serve immediately.
Spoon velouté sauce over chicken and reheat green beans or broccoli in butter just before serving.

You will find that **cooking times** given in the individual recipes for these dishes have sometimes been adapted in the timetable to help you when cooking and serving this menu as a party meal.

Appetizer

Fillets of Sole Meunière

$1\frac{1}{4}$–$1\frac{1}{2}$ lb sole fillets
$\frac{1}{4}$ cup seasoned flour (made with $\frac{1}{4}$ teaspoon salt, pinch of pepper)
4–6 slices of bacon
2 tablespoons butter

To finish
2 tablespoons butter
juice of $\frac{1}{2}$ lemon
salt and pepper
1 teaspoon chopped parsley
1 teaspoon chopped fresh herbs (chives, thyme, chervil, tarragon)

Method
Wash the sole fillets, pat dry with paper towels and coat with seasoned flour.

Fry the bacon until crisp, drain on paper towels and keep warm.

Heat a heavy frying pan, add 2 tablespoons butter and when it starts to foam put in the fish, skinned side up. Fry 2–3 minutes on each side until the fish is golden brown. Arrange the fillets overlapping on a hot serving dish with bacon slices between the fillets.

Wipe out the frying pan with paper towels, add the remaining 2 tablespoons butter and cook gently to a nut-brown (noisette). At once add the lemon juice, seasoning and herbs. Swirl the pan quickly to blend the butter and juice and, while it is still foaming, pour over the fish. Serve at once.

After washing and drying fillets of sole, coat them with seasoned flour before frying

As the butter starts to foam, put the coated fillets into the pan, skinned side up

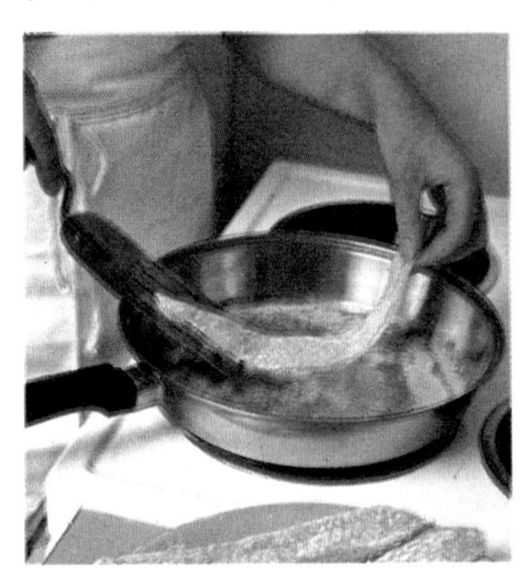

Entrée

Suprêmes de Poulet Villeroi (Chicken Suprêmes Villeroi)

2 chickens (3½–4 lb each) or 4 boned chicken breasts and 2 thighs
2–3 tablespoons white wine

For duxelles stuffing
1 shallot, finely chopped
2 tablespoons butter
2 cups (½ lb) mushrooms, finely chopped
2 tablespoons fresh white breadcrumbs
salt and pepper
1 egg white
3–4 tablespoons heavy cream

For duchesse potatoes
4 medium potatoes
3 tablespoons butter
2 egg yolks
½ cup hot milk
1 egg, beaten with ½ teaspoon salt (for glaze)

velouté sauce, made with 2 tablespoons butter, 1½ tablespoons flour, and 1½ cups chicken stock (made from chicken giblets and any chicken bones)
2 egg yolks (for liaison)
½ cup light cream (for liaison)
squeeze of lemon juice (to finish)
½ tablespoon butter (to finish)

4 large rounds of foil; pastry bag; large plain and star tubes

Method

If using whole chickens, cut white meat from breastbone to make suprêmes and discard the skin.

To make duxelles stuffing: cut meat from 2 thighs or 1 whole chicken leg, grind and reserve it. Put shallot in a skillet with the butter, cover and cook over a low heat until soft but not brown. Add chopped mushrooms, cook the mixture over high heat for 2–3 minutes or until all moisture has evaporated, then stir in breadcrumbs and seasoning. Spread on a plate to cool. Beat egg white until frothy, then beat it into the ground raw chicken a little at a time. Season with salt and stir in cream. Work into mushroom mixture and taste for seasoning.

Set oven at moderate (350°F). Split chicken suprêmes carefully to make a large pocket just above the natural division. Put stuffing in the pastry bag fitted with plain tube and fill pockets in suprêmes.

Set suprêmes on rounds of buttered foil and sprinkle with white wine. Fold over foil and seal edges to make the 'papillotes'. Bake in heated oven 45–50 minutes.

To make duchesse potato mixture: cook the potatoes in boiling salted water for 15–20 minutes or until tender, drain and dry well. Mash to a purée, return to saucepan and over low heat beat in butter, seasoning, egg yolks, and enough hot milk to make a firm purée.

Put mixture into the pastry bag fitted with large star tube and pipe border of potato around edge of a large gratin or shallow baking dish. Brush potato with the egg, bake in heated oven, above chicken, for 10–15 minutes until potato is golden brown. Take out dish and reserve it.

Make the velouté sauce, season and add liaison of egg yolks and cream. Reheat carefully without boiling and stir in lemon juice. Take from heat, adjust seasoning and beat in the ½ tablespoon butter.

Take chicken from oven, remove foil 'papillotes' and arrange stuffed chicken suprêmes, overlapping, in the gratin dish, inside potato border.

Spoon enough sauce over suprêmes to coat them and serve remaining sauce separately. Serve with buttered green beans or broccoli.

To remove chicken suprêmes, with a sharp knife cut away in one piece all of the breast meat down to the wing bone

After cutting a pocket just above the natural division in the suprême, fill with duxelles stuffing and place suprême on buttered foil

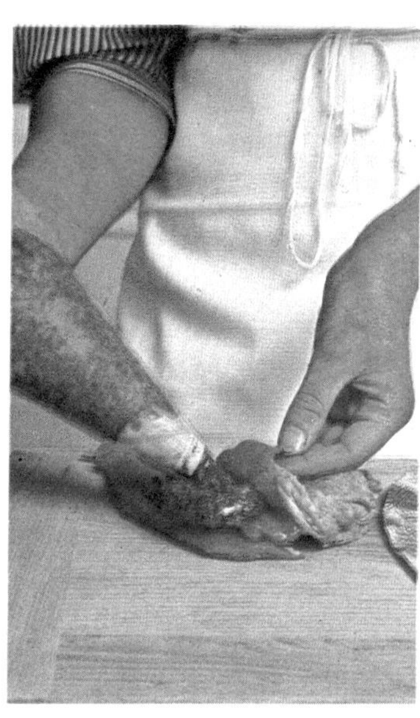

Finished dishes for an elegant dinner include from left to right: suprêmes of chicken Villeroi; fillets of sole meunière garnished with slices of crisp bacon; coffee gâteau with fruits rafraîchis

Dessert

Gâteau au Café

For Génoise sponge
3 eggs
$\frac{1}{4}$ cup unsalted butter
$\frac{1}{2}$ cup sugar
$\frac{1}{2}$ cup cake flour
pinch of salt
$\frac{1}{2}$ teaspoon vanilla
$\frac{1}{4}$ cup apricot jam glaze (to finish)

For butter cream frosting
$\frac{3}{4}$ cup unsalted butter
2 egg yolks
$\frac{1}{4}$ cup sugar
$\frac{1}{4}$ cup water
2 teaspoons dry instant coffee dissolved in a little water

For glacé icing
3 cups confectioners' sugar
4–5 tablespoons sugar syrup
1 tablespoon dry instant coffee dissolved in a little water

9 inch tube pan; pastry bag and medium star tube

Method
Set oven at moderate (350°F). Grease the tube pan and sprinkle with sugar, then flour and salt, discarding any excess.

Make the Génoise sponge cake mixture and pour the batter into the prepared pan; bake in the heated oven for 40–45 minutes or until the cake springs back when lightly touched with a fingertip. Remove from the pan after about 10 minutes and let cool on a wire rack.

Make the butter cream frosting and color and flavor it to taste with dry instant coffee.

Split the cooled cake into 3 layers, spread the layers with the butter cream frosting, reserving one-third for decoration, then sandwich the layers together. Brush the cake lightly with warm apricot jam glaze.

To prepare glacé icing: stir enough of the cold sugar syrup into the sifted confectioners' sugar to make a thick, creamy mixture. Flavor with the instant coffee and warm the icing gently. Pour over the cake and, when set, decorate with rosettes of frosting. Serve with fruits rafraîchis.

Cut the cool Génoise sponge cake into three layers; sandwich the layers together with some of the coffee-flavored butter cream frosting

After sandwiching the cake, brush tops and sides lightly with the apricot jam glaze and then cover it with coffee-flavored glacé icing

Sugar Syrup

For 1 cup: in a pan gently heat 1 cup sugar and $\frac{3}{4}$ cup water until sugar is dissolved. Bring to a boil and cook steadily for 3–4 minutes (220°F on a sugar thermometer). Cool syrup and store in a screwtop jar.

Accompaniment to dessert

Fruits Rafraîchis (Fresh Fruit Salad)

3–4 cups mixed fresh fruits – strawberries, green seedless grapes, oranges and bananas
$\frac{1}{2}$ cup sugar syrup
3–4 tablespoons kirsch (optional)

Method
Wash, hull and halve the strawberries, pull the grapes off the stems; section the oranges and peel and slice the bananas.

Combine the fruits in a glass bowl, spoon over the sugar syrup and flavor with a little kirsch, if you like. Cover and chill 2–3 hours before using. Serve in the glass bowl.

Ratatouille is a mixture of cooked peppers, zucchini and tomatoes flavored with garlic (recipe is on page 118)

INFORMAL MENUS

Take your choice from five complete informal menus all designed for easy entertaining. For an authentic supper from Provence, try some French country specialities like the delicious tomato and saffron-flavored Mediterranean fish soup that is easy to reproduce in America. Serve assorted sandwiches for a quick and delicious casual menu. Mixtures of liver sausage and chutney, tongue and curry or chicken and bacon on toast are the perfect accompaniment to a home-made vegetable soup. Or let your guests serve themselves from a simple party supper that includes shrimp and bacon kebabs and a savory rice casserole.

For a larger gathering, follow the easy timetable for the make ahead cold buffet. The tempting menu features iced pimiento and zucchini soup, three colorful salads and apricot Moscovite, a delicious molded dessert, accompanied by little praline petits fours. The make ahead hot buffet is just as simple and rewarding. Delectable crab and cheese toasts and fricassée of beef with chestnuts are rivaled by the old-fashioned homey dessert of hot apple and blackberry pie, topped with sour cream sauce.

Soup and Sandwich Snack

Vegetable Soup
Shrimp Sandwich
Ham and Cream Cheese Sandwich
Cottage Cheese and Pineapple Sandwich
Crab Meat Sandwich
Roast Beef Sandwich
Liver Sausage and Chutney Sandwich
Salami and Pickle Sandwich
Chicken and Bacon Sandwich
Tongue and Curry Sandwich

TIMETABLE

Day before
Make soup.

Two to three hours ahead
Except for toasted chicken sandwich, all sandwiches can be prepared and kept tightly covered in the refrigerator.

Short time before serving
Reheat soup.
Make toasted chicken and bacon sandwich.

Soup

Vegetable Soup

1 onion, chopped
2 carrots, diced
3 stalks of celery, thinly sliced
$\frac{1}{2}$ medium cabbage, shredded
3 tablespoons butter
6 cups chicken stock or water
salt and pepper
2 leeks, thinly sliced
1 small white turnip, diced

Method
In a kettle melt the butter, add the onion, carrots and celery, cover and cook gently for 5–7 minutes or until the butter is absorbed. Add the stock or water and seasoning, cover and simmer 20 minutes. Add the leeks and turnip and simmer 15 minutes longer. Add the cabbage, simmer 15 minutes more and taste for seasoning.

Sandwiches

Roast Beef Sandwich

For 1 sandwich: mix $\frac{1}{4}$ cup grated cooked beets with 2 teaspoons prepared horseradish and 1 tablespoon sour cream. Spread 2 slices of white bread with $\frac{1}{2}$ tablespoon butter and top 1 slice with beet mixture. Add 3–4 thin slices of roast beef, sprinkle with grated coarse salt (or regular salt) and top with the second slice of bread.

Liver Sausage and Chutney Sandwich

For 1 sandwich: mix 1 tablespoon chopped mango chutney with $\frac{1}{3}$ cup diced liver sausage. Mix 2 coarsely chopped lettuce leaves with 1 tablespoon mayonnaise. Spread 2 slices of white bread with $\frac{1}{2}$ tablespoon butter and 1 teaspoon Dijon-style mustard. Spread 1 slice with liver sausage mixture, top with lettuce mixture and cover with the second slice of bread.

Shrimp Sandwich

For 4 sandwiches: coarsely chop $\frac{1}{2}$ lb cooked peeled shrimps and mix with 3 stalks of celery, chopped, 1 dessert apple, cored and chopped (not pared), 1 tablespoon tomato ketchup and 3 tablespoons mayonnaise. Sandwich between buttered wholewheat bread.

Ham and Cream Cheese Sandwich

For 1 sandwich: spread 2 slices of dark rye bread with $\frac{1}{2}$ tablespoon butter and $\frac{1}{2}$ teaspoon hot mustard. Spread each slice with 2 tablespoons cream cheese, sprinkle 1 slice with celery salt and top with 1–2 slices of ham. Cover with the second slice of bread.

Note: for a group of four, make 3–4 types of sandwiches with contrasting ingredients so that each person has a choice.

Cottage Cheese and Pineapple Sandwich

Spread 2 slices of wholewheat bread with $\frac{1}{2}$ tablespoon butter and top each with 2 tablespoons cottage cheese. Sprinkle 1 slice with seasoning and add 1 tablespoon chopped watercress. Top with 2 tablespoons chopped drained pineapple chunks and cover with the second slice of bread.

Crab Meat Sandwich

For 1 sandwich: mix $\frac{1}{2}$ cup crab meat with 2 tablespoons mayonnaise. Spread 2 slices of wholewheat bread with mayonnaise and spread 1 with crab mixture. Top with 8–10 thin slices of cucumber, season and cover with the second slice of bread.

Salami and Pickle Sandwich

For 2 sandwiches: mix 1 slice drained canned pimiento, chopped, with 1 large dill pickle, chopped and 2 tablespoons mayonnaise. Spread 4 slices of pumpernickel bread with $\frac{1}{2}$ tablespoon butter and cover 2 slices with pickle mixture. Top with 3–4 thin slices of salami and cover with the remaining bread.

Homemade vegetable soup is a satisfying and warming appetizer for an informal menu

Chicken and Bacon Sandwich

For 1 sandwich: broil or fry 2 slices of bacon, cut in half. Mix $\frac{1}{3}$ cup chopped cooked chicken with 2 tablespoons mayonnaise. Toast 2 slices of white bread on one side, trim the crusts and spread $\frac{1}{2}$ tablespoon butter on the untoasted side. Spread 1 slice with chicken mixture, add bacon and top with the second slice of bread.

Tongue and Curry Sandwich

For 1 sandwich: mix 2 tablespoons mayonnaise with $\frac{1}{2}$ teaspoon curry powder. Spread a little mayonnaise on 2 slices of white bread and mix remaining mayonnaise with 2 coarsely chopped lettuce leaves. Spread lettuce mixture on 1 slice of bread, top with 2–3 thin slices of tongue and cover with the second slice of bread.

Toasted chicken and bacon sandwich is just one of many sandwiches for a quick and casual menu

A Provençal Supper

Soupe de Poisson
(Fish Soup)

Spaghetti Grimaldi

Ratatouille

Figues au Fromage Frais
(Figs with Cream Cheese)

TIMETABLE

Day before
Make the soup, cover and keep in refrigerator.
Make aioli, cover and keep in refrigerator.
Make ratatouille, cover and keep in refrigerator.

In morning
Make anchovy and olive mixture for spaghetti and leave in saucepan, covered, ready to toss spaghetti.
Make cheese filling for figs and keep covered.
Wash lettuce leaves, if using, and keep in plastic bag in refrigerator.

Half hour before serving
Fill figs with cheese and arrange on platter. Serve at room temperature.
Bake croûtes for soup.

Quarter hour before serving
Cook spaghetti, drain, rinse and leave in 1–2 inches warm water.
If serving the ratatouille hot, reheat gently on top of stove.
Reheat soup.

After serving soup
Drain spaghetti and toss with anchovy and olive mixture.
Transfer the ratatouille to serving dish.

Soupe au Poisson

(Fish Soup)

2 lb white fish, including skin and bone (bass, red snapper, perch, scup, bluefish)
$\frac{1}{2}$ cup olive oil
1 onion, chopped
2 cloves of garlic, crushed
1 tomato, peeled, seeded and chopped or $\frac{1}{2}$ cup tomato purée
1 branch fresh fennel or 1 teaspoon fennel seeds, crushed
1 bay leaf
1 teaspoon thyme
large pinch of saffron soaked in $\frac{1}{4}$ cup boiling water for 20 minutes
2 quarts water
salt
black pepper, freshly ground

For serving
2–3 long crusty rolls or 1 thin loaf of French bread
$\frac{1}{2}$ cup grated Parmesan cheese
aioli (garlic mayonnaise)

Method
Wash the fish thoroughly and cut in 2 inch pieces.

In a kettle heat half the oil and fry the onion until just beginning to brown. Add the garlic, tomato or tomato purée, fennel, bay leaf and thyme and cook, stirring, for 2–3 minutes.

Add the fish, pour over the water, saffron with its liquid and the remaining oil and season. Cover, bring to a boil and boil steadily for 15 minutes.

Watchpoint: unlike most fish dishes, soupe au poisson must be boiled so the oil emulsifies with the water.

To make croûtes: cut the rolls or bread in $\frac{1}{2}$ inch diagonal slices, set them on a baking sheet and bake in a moderate oven (350°F) for 10–15 minutes or until lightly browned.

Strain the soup, pressing the fish and vegetables well to extract all the liquid. Flake about 2 cups fish from the bones and purée it in a blender with a little of the fish liquid or work it through a food mill. Stir the remaining fish liquid into the purée, return the soup to the pan and reheat it. Taste for seasoning – the soup should be quite spicy – and serve with bread croûtes, aioli and Parmesan cheese.

The soup is normally served in a tureen. The croûtes are spread with aioli and placed in bowls, then the soup is spooned over them and the cheese is sprinkled on top.

Aioli

(Garlic Mayonnaise)

4 cloves of garlic, crushed
2 egg yolks
salt
black pepper, freshly ground
1 cup olive oil
juice of $\frac{1}{2}$ lemon

Aioli can also be made in a blender as for regular mayonnaise (see Volume 4).

Method
Beat the egg yolks with garlic and seasoning in a bowl until the mixture is thick and the garlic is completely puréed. Add the oil drop by drop, beating constantly; when 2 tablespoons of oil have been added the mixture should be very thick. Stir in 1 teaspoon lemon juice.

Continue adding the oil a little faster, beating constantly, until all is added. Stir in the remaining lemon juice with seasoning to taste.

Spaghetti Grimaldi

1 lb spaghetti
$\frac{1}{4}$ cup olive oil
5 anchovy fillets, soaked in a little milk to remove salt, drained and chopped
1 tablespoon capers, chopped
$\frac{1}{4}$ cup ripe Italian-style olives, pitted and chopped
1 teaspoon oregano
2 cloves of garlic, crushed (optional)
black pepper, freshly ground
salt
$\frac{1}{2}$ cup grated Parmesan cheese (for serving)

Method

Cook the spaghetti in plenty of boiling water for 8–10 minutes or until almost tender ('al dente'); drain and rinse it with hot water.

In a saucepan put the oil, anchovy fillets, capers, olives, oregano and garlic, if used, and cook gently for 1 minute. Add the spaghetti with plenty of black pepper and toss over the heat until very hot. Taste for seasoning – salt may not be needed because the anchovies are salty.

Pile the spaghetti mixture in a bowl and serve grated Parmesan cheese separately.

Ratatouille

$\frac{1}{4}$ cup olive oil
1 onion, chopped
2 green peppers, cored, seeded and chopped
2 red bell peppers, cored, seeded and chopped
3 medium zucchini, thinly sliced
1 eggplant, diced (optional)
4–5 Italian-style plum tomatoes, drained and chopped
2 cloves of garlic, crushed
1 teaspoon ground coriander
salt
black pepper, freshly ground

Method

If using eggplant, sprinkle it with salt to draw out the bitter juices (dégorger), let stand 15 minutes, rinse with cold water and drain.

In a skillet or shallow flameproof casserole heat the oil and fry the onion until golden brown. Add the peppers, zucchini, tomatoes, eggplant, if used, garlic, coriander and seasoning and mix well.

Cover and cook over low heat for 5 minutes until the vegetables begin to soften. Stir well and cook, uncovered, 8–10 minutes longer or until the vegetables are tender, stirring occasionally. Taste for seasoning and serve hot or cold.

Figues au Fromage Frais
(Figs with Cream Cheese)

12–14 fresh figs
1 package (8 oz) cream cheese
4–6 tablespoons heavy cream
$\frac{1}{4}$ cup sugar
little paprika (for sprinkling)
few lettuce leaves (for garnish) – optional

Pastry bag and large star tube

Method

Cut the figs almost in quarters, leaving them joined at the base. Beat the cream cheese with enough cream to make a soft mixture; beat in the sugar.

Put the mixture in a pastry bag fitted with a star tube and pipe the cheese into the center of the figs.

For serving, set the figs on lettuce leaves, if you like, and sprinkle lightly with paprika.

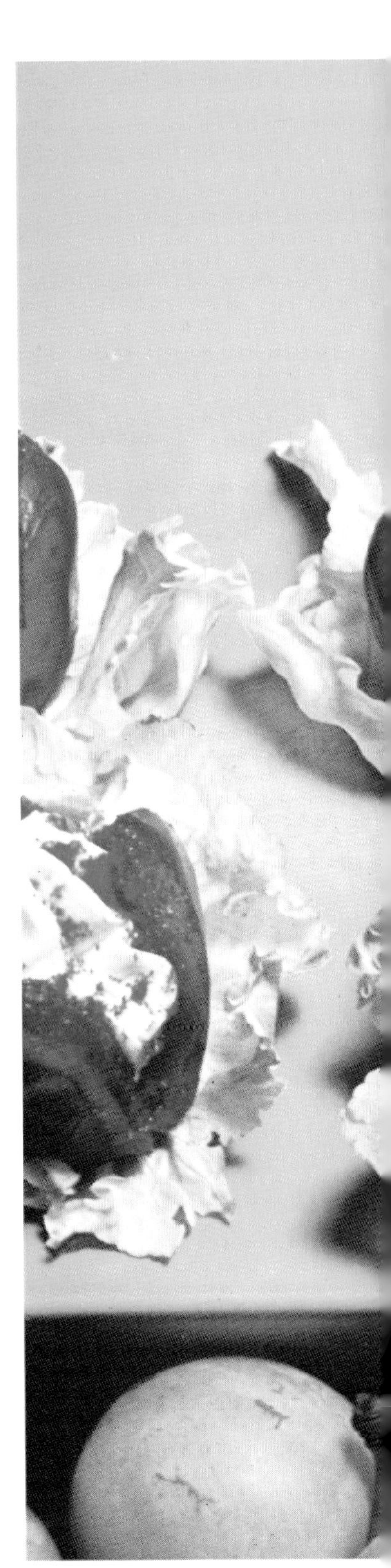

Figs with cream cheese are sprinkled with paprika and served on individual lettuce leaves

Make Ahead Cold Buffet

Iced Pimiento and Zucchini Soup

Italian Turkey Salad

Potato Salad

Cherry Tomato Salad

Apricot Moscovite

Pains de Seigle (Praline Petits Fours)

TIMETABLE

Several days ahead
Make pains de seigle and store in airtight container.

Day before
Make soup and keep covered in refrigerator; make garnish and keep in refrigerator.
Make dressing for turkey, potato and tomato salads.
Make mayonnaise for potato salad.
Cook apricots and make custard for apricot Moscovite. Cover and store in refrigerator.

In morning
Make mushroom mixture for turkey salad and cut up turkey; keep in refrigerator in separate containers.
Peel tomatoes and keep covered; wash watercress or lettuce and keep in plastic bag.
Make potato salad and keep covered.,
Prepare apricot Moscovite, cover tightly in the mold and chill; make sauce.

Short time before serving
Unmold apricot Moscovite, whip cream and decorate. Keep with sauce separately in refrigerator.
Complete turkey salad.
Complete tomato salad.
Stir garnish into soup.

Iced Pimiento and Zucchini Soup

4 slices of canned pimiento, drained and chopped
1 lb zucchini
4 cups chicken stock
4–5 scallions, chopped
2 tablespoons butter
salt and pepper

Method
Peel the zucchini and cut one in $\frac{1}{2}$ inch pieces. Chop the remaining zucchini. Simmer the zucchini pieces in 1 cup of the stock for 6–8 minutes or until almost tender, add 2–3 tablespoons green part of the scallions and cook 1 minute longer. Drain the vegetables, reserving the stock.

In a kettle melt the butter and fry the chopped zucchini and remaining scallions over low heat until soft but not brown. Add the chicken stock, including the reserved stock, the pimiento (reserving 2 tablespoons for garnish) and seasoning, cover and simmer 10–15 minutes. Purée the soup in a blender or work it through a food mill, cover it and chill.

A short time before serving, stir in the cooked zucchini and scallions with the chopped pimiento and taste for seasoning.

Iced pimiento and zucchini soup is a simple dish to make for a cold buffet

Italian Turkey Salad

2–3 cups cooked turkey, cut in pieces
1 can (15 oz) artichoke hearts, drained, or 1 package frozen artichokes, cooked
1 $\frac{1}{2}$ cups ($\frac{1}{3}$ lb) mushrooms, thinly sliced

For dressing
$\frac{3}{4}$ cup olive oil
grated rind and juice of 1 lemon
salt
black pepper, freshly ground
1 teaspoon oregano
2 tablespoons chopped Italian parsley (fresh coriander)

Method

To make the dressing: whisk the lemon juice with salt and pepper until the salt is dissolved. Gradually whisk in the oil, so the dressing emulsifies, and add the lemon rind and oregano. Stir in the mushrooms, cover and stand at least $\frac{1}{2}$ hour or up to 4 hours to marinate.

Mix the turkey and artichoke hearts, quartered, in a bowl and spoon over the mushrooms and dressing. Sprinkle with Italian parsley, cover and let stand $\frac{1}{2}$ hour before serving.

Cherry Tomato Salad

1 pint cherry tomatoes, peeled
bunch of watercress or few leaves of lettuce
$\frac{1}{4}$ cup vinaigrette dressing
1 clove garlic, crushed (optional)
1 tablespoon chopped parsley

Method

Arrange the lettuce leaves around a salad bowl and pile cherry tomatoes in the center, or arrange sprigs of watercress around the tomatoes. Stir the parsley and garlic, if used, into the dressing and spoon it over the tomatoes.

Vinaigrette Dressing

For $\frac{1}{4}$ cup: mix 1 tablespoon vinegar (any of the following types: red or white wine, cider or tarragon) with $\frac{1}{4}$ teaspoon salt and $\frac{1}{4}$ teaspoon freshly ground black pepper. Gradually add 3 tablespoons olive or peanut oil, whisking until the dressing thickens slightly. Taste for seasoning. Chopped fresh herbs (thyme, marjoram, basil or parsley) are an excellent addition, as is a pinch of sugar, according to your taste.

Potato Salad

4–5 medium potatoes
$\frac{1}{4}$ cup vinaigrette dressing
salt and pepper
1 cup mayonnaise
1–2 tablespoons light cream or milk
$\frac{1}{2}$ teaspoon paprika
8–12 ripe olives (for garnish) – optional

Method

Cook potatoes in their skins in boiling salted water for 15 minutes or until just tender; do not overcook or they will break up when sliced and tossed in dressing. While still hot, peel potatoes, cut into slices, add the vinaigrette dressing (potatoes will absorb it), season, cover and cool.

When cold, mix in 2–3 tablespoons mayonnaise and pile the potatoes in a bowl. Thin the remaining mayonnaise with a little cream or milk and coat the potatoes. Sprinkle with paprika and decorate with halved pitted olives, if you like. Cover and serve within 1–2 hours.

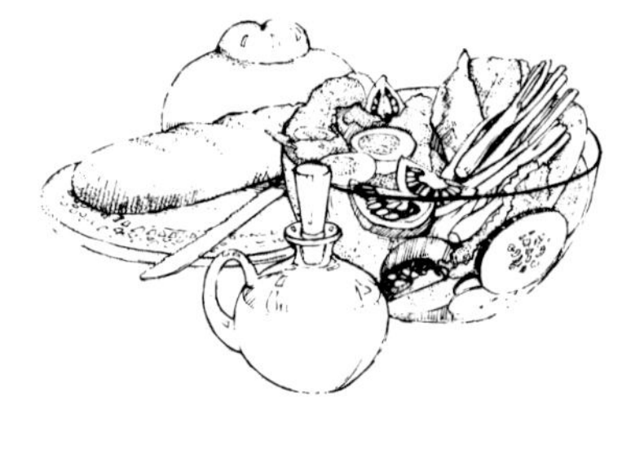

Mayonnaise

2 egg yolks
salt and pepper
pinch of dry mustard
$\frac{3}{4}$ cup oil
2 tablespoons wine vinegar

Makes about 1 cup.

Method

Beat egg yolks and seasonings until thick in a bowl with a small whisk or wooden spoon, or use an electric mixer. Add the oil drop by drop, beating constantly. When 2 tablespoons of oil have been added, mixture should be very thick. Stir in 1 teaspoon of vinegar.

The remaining oil can be added a little more quickly, either 1 tablespoon at a time and beaten well between each addition until it is absorbed, or in a thin steady stream if using an electric mixer.

When all the oil has been incorporated, add remaining vinegar to taste, with extra salt and pepper as necessary.

To thin and lighten mayonnaise, add a little hot water.

Watchpoint: mayonnaise curdles easily so remember the following points.

1 Eggs should be at room temperature, not chilled.

2 If oil is cold or appears cloudy, warm it slightly over a pan of hot water.

3 Add oil drop by drop at first and continue adding it very slowly. If mayonnaise will no longer thicken or starts to separate, stop adding oil and beat well. If mayonnaise separates slightly, beat in 1 tablespoon boiling water.

4 If mayonnaise curdles, start with a fresh yolk in another bowl. Beat well with seasoning, then add curdled mixture very slowly, as for the oil. When curdled mixture is completely added, more oil can be beaten in if the mixture is too thin.

For apricot Moscovite, pipe rosettes of whipped cream onto the apricot mold

Apricot Moscovite

½ lb fresh apricots, halved and pitted, or ½ lb (1½ cups) dried apricots, soaked if necessary according to package directions and drained
sugar syrup (made with 1½ cups water and ½ cup sugar)
1 envelope gelatin
1½ cups milk
3 egg yolks
⅓ cup sugar
1 cup heavy cream, whipped until it holds a soft shape
3–4 tablespoons brandy (optional)

For decoration
½ cup heavy cream, stiffly whipped
1 tablespoon praline powder (see box)

Plain or fluted ring mold (5 cup capacity); pastry bag and medium star tube

Method

Lightly oil the ring mold.

Add the fresh or dried apricots to the sugar syrup and poach 10–15 minutes or until tender; let cool.

Drain the apricots, reserving the syrup; work the fruit through a sieve to make a purée, or purée it in a blender. Divide the purée in half and chill one half in the refrigerator. Sprinkle gelatin over one-third of a cup of apricot syrup and let stand 5 minutes until spongy.

Scald the milk, beat the egg yolks with the sugar until they start to thicken and gradually stir in the hot milk. Pour the custard mixture into a pan and cook over a low heat, stirring constantly, until it coats the back of a spoon; do not let it boil. Strain into a bowl, add the softened gelatin and stir until dissolved.

Mix the chilled apricot purée with the lightly whipped cream. Set the custard mixture over a pan of ice water and stir until on the point of setting. Fold in the apricot cream mixture and flavor with 1–2 tablespoons brandy. Pour into the prepared mold and chill 2 hours or until set. Flavor the remaining apricot purée with the remaining brandy and stir in enough of the reserved syrup to make a sauce.

A short time before serving, turn the apricot Moscovite out onto a platter. Put the stiffly whipped cream into the pastry bag fitted with the star tube and decorate the mold with rosettes of cream. Sprinkle praline on top and pour the sauce around the base of the mold. Serve with pains de seigle petits four (see recipe on page 125).

Praline Powder

For ⅔ cup: put ⅔ cup whole unblanched almonds and ⅔ cup sugar in a heavy-based pan. Cook over low heat until the sugar melts, shaking pan occasionally. When the sugar turns a pale golden brown, stir the mixture with a metal spoon and continue cooking until it is dark brown, but do not let it burn. Pour at once onto an oiled baking sheet; leave until cold and hard. Grind in a rotary cheese grater or a grinder or work in a blender a little at a time.

Praline powder can be stored in an airtight container – it may become soft and sticky, but the flavor will not be impaired.

Apricot Moscovite is decorated with rosettes of cream and praline. Serve with pains de seigle petits fours

Pains de Seigle (Praline Petits Fours)

- ½ cup praline powder – see box on page 123
- 1 cup whole blanched almonds, ground
- ½ cup sugar
- 3 tablespoons flour
- 2 egg whites, beaten until frothy
- confectioners' sugar (for rolling)

Non-stick silicone paper

Pains de seigle (rye breads) are named because they resemble the color of rye bread. Makes about 24 petits fours.

Method

Set oven at moderate (350°F).

Mix ground almonds, sugar and flour together and work through a coarse sieve. Moisten the almond mixture with about three-quarters of the lightly beaten egg whites, adding the egg whites gradually and pounding the mixture thoroughly to bind it together. Work in the praline powder.

Divide the mixture into small balls the size of a walnut, roll them in the remaining beaten egg white, then in confectioners' sugar. Place on silicone paper on a baking sheet and bake in heated oven for about 15–20 minutes or until lightly browned.

Transfer petits fours to a wire rack to cool and store up to a week in an airtight container.

Before baking the pains de seigle, roll them in egg white, then in confectioners' sugar

Make Ahead Hot Buffet

Crab and Cheese Toasts

Fricassée of Beef with Chestnuts

Orange Baked Potatoes

Blackberry and Apple Pie with Sour Cream Sauce

TIMETABLE

Day before
Make fricassée of beef and keep in refrigerator.
Stuff potatoes but do not bake; keep covered in refrigerator.

In morning
Make crab and cheese toasts but do not brown; keep covered in refrigerator.
Prepare apple pie, cover with pastry but do not bake; keep covered in refrigerator.
Make sour cream sauce and chill.

One hour before serving
Set oven at moderately hot (375°F).

Thirty to forty minutes before serving
Bake blackberry and apple pie.
Put potatoes in oven to brown.

Short time before serving
Reheat fricassée on top of stove.
Broil cheese and crab toasts.
Turn down oven to low to keep beef fricassée, potatoes and blackberry and apple pie warm while serving toasts.

Crab and Cheese Toasts

- 1 cup (½ lb) crab meat
- 4 slices of Gruyère cheese, each cut crosswise in 4
- ⅓ cup fresh white breadcrumbs
- 1 egg, beaten to mix
- 2–3 tablespoons heavy cream
- ¼ teaspoon dry mustard
- pinch of cayenne or few drops of Tabasco
- dash of Worcestershire sauce
- salt and pepper
- 4 slices of white bread, toasted and crusts removed

The toasts can be prepared up to 6 hours ahead.

Method

Mix the crab meat with the breadcrumbs, egg, cream, seasonings and plenty of salt and pepper – the mixture should be quite spicy. Cut the slices of toast in half and spread them with the crab mixture. Top with 2 slices of cheese, cover tightly and chill.

Just before serving, broil the toasts until the cheese begins to brown.

For an unusual hot buffet dish, serve fricassée of beef with chestnuts

Fricassée of Beef with Chestnuts

$1\frac{1}{2}$–2 lb round or chuck steak, cut in $1\frac{1}{2}$-inch cubes
$\frac{3}{4}$–1 lb chestnuts, peeled
3 tablespoons olive oil
$\frac{1}{4}$ cup brandy
1 onion, sliced
black pepper, freshly ground
$\frac{1}{2}$ lb piece of bacon or salt pork
2 tablespoons flour
2 cups red wine
salt
bouquet garni, including a stalk of celery
1 clove of garlic, crushed
12–16 baby onions, peeled
$1\frac{1}{2}$–2 cups stock

Method

In a bowl (not aluminum) mix the beef with the olive oil, brandy and sliced onion with plenty of freshly ground black pepper. Cover and let marinate 8–12 hours in the refrigerator, stirring occasionally. Drain the beef and pat dry with paper towels, reserving any marinade.

Blanch the bacon or salt pork in boiling water for 35–40 minutes, drain it, discard skin and cut in cubes.

In a flameproof casserole cook the bacon or salt pork, stirring, until browned. Remove it and brown the beef on all sides, a few pieces at a time. Stir in the flour and cook until browned. At once pour in the wine and add the bouquet garni, bacon, garlic, reserved marinade and salt. Cover and cook in a moderately low oven (325°F) for $1–1\frac{1}{2}$ hours or until the beef is almost tender. Add the baby onions and cook $\frac{1}{2}$ hour longer or until the beef and onions are tender.

Meanwhile simmer the chestnuts in stock for 25–30 minutes or until tender and drain them. Stir the chestnuts carefully into the beef mixture, taste for seasoning and serve with orange baked potatoes.

Orange Baked Potatoes

4 large baking potatoes
$\frac{1}{4}$ cup butter
about $\frac{1}{4}$ cup light cream
grated rind of 1 orange

Pastry bag and large star tube (optional)

Method

Scrub the potatoes well, dry with paper towels and roll in salt; prick them with a fork. Bake in a moderate oven (350°F) for $1\frac{1}{4}–1\frac{1}{2}$ hours or until tender.

Cut off the tops of the potatoes, lengthwise, scoop out the pulp and mash. Beat in the butter, cream, orange rind and salt and pepper.

If you like, put the potato mixture into a pastry bag, fitted with a large star tube, and pipe the mixture into the potato shells, making rosettes on top. Alternatively, fill the mixture into the potato shells and roughen the tops with a fork. Bake in a hot oven (400°F) for 10 minutes or until the potatoes are golden brown.

If preparing potatoes in advance, cover them and keep in the refrigerator for up to 24 hours. Bake in a moderate oven (350°F) for 20–25 minutes or until browned.

Apple and Blackberry Pie

$1\frac{1}{2}$ lb tart apples
1 pint fresh blackberries or 1 can (16 oz) blackberries, drained
$\frac{1}{2}$–$\frac{2}{3}$ cups sugar
1 tablespoon cornstarch
1 tablespoon lemon juice
1 tablespoon butter
granulated sugar (for sprinkling)

For pie pastry
$1\frac{1}{2}$ cups flour
pinch of salt
$\frac{1}{4}$ cup butter
$\frac{1}{4}$ cup shortening
2–3 tablespoons cold water

Shallow baking dish or 9 inch pie pan

Method

Make pastry dough and chill it 15 minutes. Set oven at moderately hot (375°F).

Pare, core and slice the apples and mix with the blackberries, sugar and cornstarch. Spread the mixture in a shallow baking dish or pie pan. Sprinkle the top with lemon juice and dot with butter.

Roll out two-thirds of the pastry dough and cover the pie. Roll out the remaining dough and cut it into 4 long strips. Arrange 1 strip in a zigzag, in a catty-corner, and set a second strip on top, overlapping it also in a zigzag so as to resemble a braid. Repeat the arrangement with the remaining strips of dough in the reverse catty-corner.

Bake the pie in the heated oven for 35–40 minutes or until the pastry is browned and the apples in the center of the pie are tender when tested with a skewer. Sprinkle with granulated sugar and serve hot with sour cream sauce separately.

Sour Cream Sauce

Whip $\frac{1}{2}$ cup heavy cream until it holds a soft shape, then stir in $\frac{1}{2}$ cup sour cream and 1 teaspoon sugar (or to taste).

Apple and blackberry pie makes a mouth-watering dessert. Serve sour cream sauce separately *(recipe is on page 127)*

A Simple Party Supper

Shrimp and Bacon Kebabs

Casserole of Squash

Savory Saffron Rice

Fresh Fruit with Cheese Cream

Almond Wafers

TIMETABLE

Day before
Add marinade to shrimps and keep, covered, in refrigerator. Prepare the squash casserole but do not bake; keep covered in refrigerator.
Cook rice and leave in casserole ready for reheating; keep in refrigerator.
Prepare almond wafer dough, wrap, and chill.

Morning
Drain the shrimps, prepare the kebabs and keep covered in refrigerator. Bake almond wafers and keep in airtight container.

Three quarters of an hour before serving
Set oven at moderate (350°F).
Make cheese cream and arrange fruit and wafers on platters.

Half hour before serving
Put rice and squash in oven to reheat.

Fifteen minutes before serving
Turn on broiler; take out rice and squash casseroles, if necessary, or turn oven to low.
Broil the shrimps.
Transfer the rice to a serving dish; serve squash in the casserole.

Shrimp and Bacon Kebabs

$1\frac{1}{2}$ lb peeled, uncooked large shrimps
$\frac{3}{4}$ lb sliced bacon

For marinade
$\frac{1}{2}$ cup white wine
$\frac{1}{4}$ cup oil
1 teaspoon oregano
1 bay leaf
black pepper, freshly ground

8 kebab skewers

Method
Combine the ingredients for the marinade, pour over the shrimps in a bowl (not aluminum), cover and chill 6–8 hours or overnight.

Cut the bacon slices in half. Drain the shrimps, discard the bay leaf and roll each shrimp in a piece of bacon. Thread the shrimps on the kebab skewers and broil them for 4–5 minutes on each side or until the bacon is crisp and browned. Serve at once.

Casserole of Squash

$1\frac{1}{2}$ lb summer squash or zucchini, sliced, or
2 butternut or acorn squash, peeled, seeds discarded and cut in large cubes
salt
3 scallions, chopped
2 tablespoons butter
1 teaspoon thyme or marjoram
black pepper, freshly ground
1 cup sour cream
$\frac{1}{4}$ cup browned breadcrumbs (for sprinkling)

Method

Cook the squash in boiling salted water for 8–12 minutes or until almost tender and drain. Sauté the scallions in the butter until soft but not browned.

In a buttered casserole, arrange the squash in layers with the scallions, sprinkle each layer with the herb and black pepper and spoon over a little sour cream. Cover the top with the remaining sour cream and sprinkle with breadcrumbs. Bake in a moderate oven (350°F) for 15–20 minutes or until the casserole is very hot and bubbling.

Savory Saffron Rice

$1\frac{1}{4}$ cups rice
2 tablespoons oil
1 onion, chopped
juice of 1 orange
1 tablespoon tomato paste
1 cup ($\frac{1}{4}$ lb) mushrooms, chopped
2 cups chicken stock
1 green pepper, cored, seeded and chopped
pinch of saffron soaked in 2 tablespoons boiling water for 20 minutes
salt and pepper

To finish
paprika (for sprinkling)
1 orange, sliced

Method

In a large flameproof casserole heat the oil and fry the onion until soft but not browned. Add the rice and cook, stirring, until it looks transparent. Stir the orange juice into the tomato paste and add to the rice with the mushrooms, stock, green pepper, saffron and its water, and seasoning. Cover, bring to boil and cook in a moderate oven (350°F) for 20 minutes.

Let stand 10 minutes, then stir with a fork and pile in a serving dish. Sprinkle the rice with paprika and arrange the orange slices around the edge.

Fresh Fruits with Cheese Cream

selection of fresh fruits – strawberries, peaches, apricots, pitted grapes, pitted cherries, plums, pears, pineapple
2 packages (3 oz each) cream cheese
$\frac{3}{4}$ cup heavy cream
brown sugar or granulated sugar (for serving)

Method

Wash the strawberries only if necessary, wipe the peaches, apricots and pears with a damp cloth; peel the pineapple and cut in chunks, discarding the core. Pile all the prepared fruits in a bowl, with pineapple separately, if using.

Beat $\frac{1}{4}$ cup heavy cream into the cream cheese until soft. Stiffly whip the remaining cream and fold into the cream cheese mixture. Pile in a bowl for serving.

Pass a bowl of brown or granulated sugar separately and let guests help themselves to fruit, cream and sugar. Serve with almond wafers.

Almond Wafers

2 cups flour
2 teaspoons ground cinnamon
$\frac{1}{2}$ teaspoon ground nutmeg
$\frac{1}{2}$ teaspoon ground allspice
1 cup butter
1 cup dark brown sugar
$\frac{1}{4}$ cup sour cream
$\frac{1}{2}$ cup sliced almonds

$2\frac{1}{2}$ inch fluted cookie cutter

Makes about 30 wafers.

Method

Sift together the flour and spices. Cream the butter, gradually beat in the sugar and continue beating until the mixture is soft and fluffy. Stir in the flour mixture alternately with the sour cream.

Shape the dough into a roll $2\frac{1}{2}$ inches thick, wrap it tightly in wax paper and chill 4–5 hours or until firm. The dough can be stored up to 2 weeks in the refrigerator or it can be frozen.

Set the oven at moderate (350°F).

Cut the thinnest possible slices from the roll and trim the edges with the cookie cutter. Set the slices on a baking sheet, scatter each one with a few sliced almonds and bake in the heated oven for 10 minutes or until lightly browned. Transfer the wafers to a wire rack to cool.

Savory saffron rice is decorated with slices of orange

MEASURING & MEASUREMENTS

The recipe quantities in the Course are measured in standard level teaspoons, tablespoons and cups and their equivalents are shown below. Any liquid pints and quarts also refer to U.S. standard measures.

When measuring dry ingredients, fill the cup or spoon to overflowing without packing down and level the top with a knife. All the dry ingredients, including flour, should be measured before sifting, although sifting may be called for later in the instructions.

Butter and margarine usually come in measured sticks (1 stick equals ½ cup) and other bulk fats can be measured by displacement. For ⅓ cup fat, fill the measuring cup ⅔ full of water. Add fat until the water reaches the 1 cup mark. Drain the cup of water and the fat remaining equals ⅓ cup.

For liquids, fill the measure to the brim, or to the calibration line.

Often quantities of seasonings cannot be stated exactly, for ingredients vary in the amount they require. The instructions 'add to taste' are literal, for it is impossible to achieve just the right balance of flavors in many dishes without tasting them.

Liquid measure	Volume equivalent
3 teaspoons	1 tablespoon
2 tablespoons	1 fluid oz
4 tablespoons	¼ cup
16 tablespoons	1 cup or 8 fluid oz
2 cups	1 pint
2 pints	1 quart
4 quarts	1 gallon

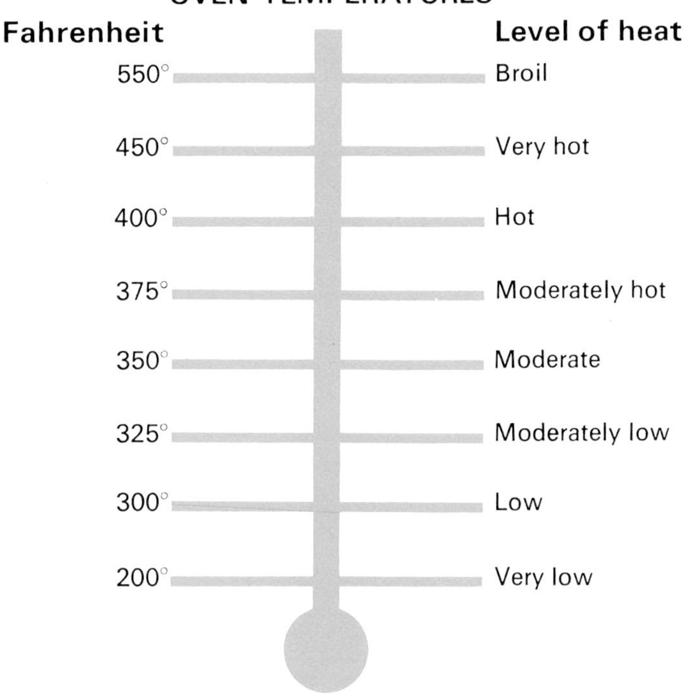

OVEN TEMPERATURES AND SHELF POSITIONS

Throughout the Cooking Course, oven temperatures are stated in degrees Fahrenheit and in generally agreed levels of heat such as 'high' and 'moderate'. The equivalents are shown on the table above.

However, exact temperature varies in different parts of an oven and the thermostat reading refers to the heat in the middle. As the oven temperature at top and bottom can vary as much as 25°F from this setting, the positioning of shelves is very important. In general, heat rises, so the hottest part of the oven is at the top, but consult the manufacturer's handbook about your individual model.

Pans and dishes of food should be placed parallel with burners or elements to avoid scorched edges.

When baking cakes, there must be room for the heat to circulate in the oven around baking sheets and cake pans; otherwise the underside of the cakes will burn. If baking more than one cake in an oven that has back burners or elements, arrange the cakes side by side. If the oven has side burners, arrange cakes back and front.

Oven thermostats are often inaccurate and are unreliable at extremely high or low temperatures. If you do a great deal of baking or question the accuracy of your oven, use a separate oven thermometer as a check on the thermostat.

Cooking Curiosities

French cooking as we know it started with the Italians. Catherine de Medici, the teenage Italian princess who married Henry II, brought with her a team of chefs who introduced to France the lavish banquets that were customary in Italy. Eating in quantity became so popular, that when the country suffered a poor harvest one year, and all meals were reduced to three courses (each course containing about 12 dishes), the nobility was outraged!

Louis XVI was also an enormous eater, although he had very little knowledge of food. On his wedding night, he ate so much that he almost choked to death and he even is known to have sat down to a grand dinner the night he was condemned to death.

Napoleon is said to have drunk over half a dozen bottles of wine for breakfast every morning and his hours for eating were so unpredictable that his chef had a fresh roast chicken prepared every fifteen minutes all day.

One of the heartiest eaters was the aunt of the well-known gourmet Brillat-Savarin who, as she lay dying in her bed while finishing a lavish dinner, thought the end would approach too soon and said: 'Quick, bring me my dessert and coffee.'

(Volume 14)

Index

E

F

G

HI

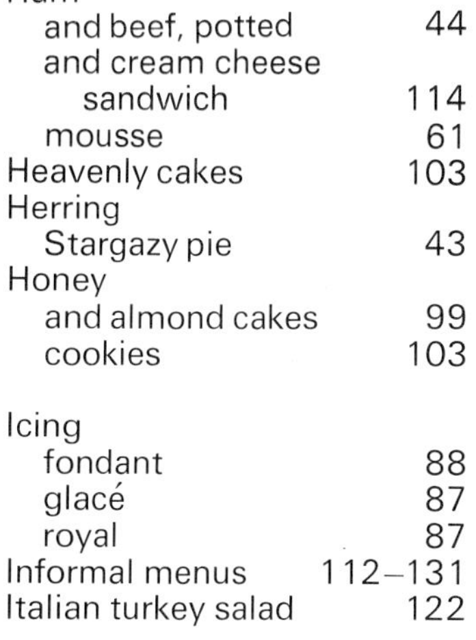

KL

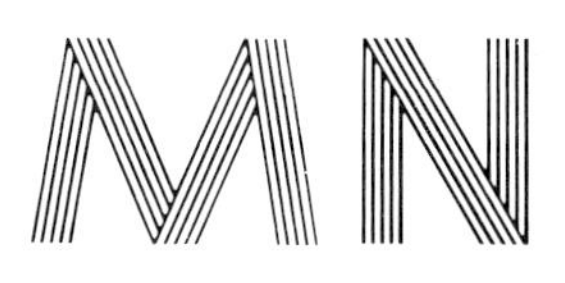

MN

O

P

R

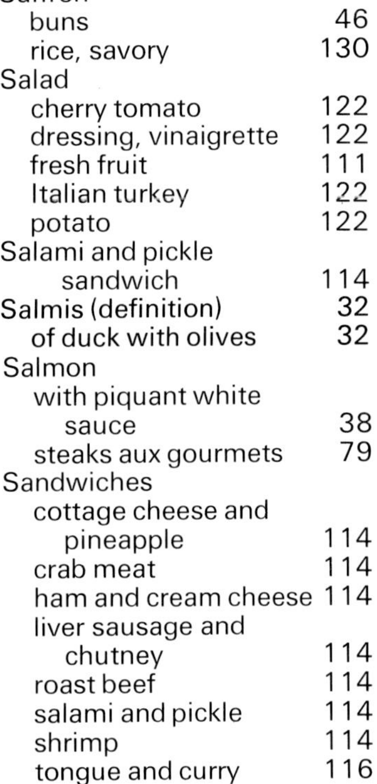

S

Index

VW

YZ

Acknowledgements
Photograph by Fred J. Maroon on page 31. Other photographs by Michael Leale and John Ledger.

NOTES